LIGHT *from the* HOLY HILLS

AMBASSADOR

LIGHT *from the* HOLY HILLS

*Lessons from
Old Testament Mountains*

by

KENNETH MOODY-STUART, MA

Light from the Holy Hills
First published 1904

ISBN   1   898787   04   2

AMBASSADOR PRODUCTIONS LTD.,
Providence House,
16 Hillview Avenue,
Belfast, BT5 6JR

Contents

LIGHT FROM THE HOLY HILLS.

I.

Mount Ararat

The Mountain of the Ark.

GENESIS viii. 4.

THE Psalmist has said, in one of the best-known and best-loved psalms, " I will lift up mine eyes unto the hills." The sacred poet sees in the mountains to which he lifted up his eyes, whether in present vision or in the vivid presentation of memory, monuments of what the Lord had done for his people in other days, and of what He would again do and be to his people in days to come. And the brilliant light that streams from the scenes that were enacted on each of those Bible Hills, shines both as a beacon and a guiding light to the pilgrim on life's journey; while by its power to search the heart, and reveal to us our position relative to the past and the future, to our duty and our destiny, it may not inaptly be termed a search-light.

The first mountain mentioned in Holy Writ is Mount ARARAT. Ararat seems to be the designation of the whole province of the Armenian highlands; but the name is specially assigned to the loftiest mountain of Armenia, the higher of whose twin peaks rises to the great altitude of over 17,000 feet—somewhat higher than Mont Blanc.

Mount Ararat is one of the most imposing of mountains, as it rises in sublime majesty 14,000 feet above the plain of the Aras or Araxes. The last 4,000 feet are covered by perpetual snow; and the summit, forming a small cruciform platform about 200 feet in diameter, is composed of eternal ice unbroken by rock. Immense avalanches of ice are frequently hurled down the mountain. Even in modern times it has been the scene of volcanic eruptions, there being on one side of the Greater Ararat a crater-like chasm—so that while it testifies to the salvation of the world from destruction by the Deluge, it also reminds the spectator of its coming doom by fire.

This mountain has an important message for the world. It testifies that Jehovah is the God of the whole earth; that He had providential and gracious dealings with the sons of men long before He chose the seed of Abraham as his peculiar people ; and that in the revelation which He has given us He has spoken to all races of mankind. Ararat, with dark storm-clouds often hovering over its hoary head, speaks to men of mercy and judgment ; and as we contemplate its majesty and its history we are constrained to exclaim : " Thy righteousness is like the great mountains ; thy judgments are a great deep. O Lord, Thou preservest man and beast. How precious is thy lovingkindness, O God; therefore the children of men put their trust under the shadow of thy wings."

It has been said that almost all painters, whether with brush or pen, have depicted ocean storms as viewed from the shore. In describing the Flood the reverse course has generally been followed. Most painters, poets, and preachers, have depicted it as viewed from the ark borne upon the face of the waters ; but Moses, its earliest narrator, gives us a view of it from the shore after it was over, from the slopes of Ararat, where the ark of Noah stranded, as the waters were abating.

Traditions of the Deluge are found in all lands and among all races; and as it is impossible that there could have been a multiplicity of deluges, all bearing the same character and having the same issue, viz., the deliverance from a watery tomb of one family of the human race, this fact proves that the race of mankind now found settled in the most remote portions of our globe, and many of them claiming to be indigenous to these regions, really sprang, as inspired history teaches, from a common stock, located in some central region where this memorable event happened, and whence after its occurrence they spread themselves over the face of the earth.

The tradition, however, of the Deluge which is embodied in the inspired record, is the fullest of all the traditions; and moral causes are assigned to it, and Divine interpositions recorded, which place it on a higher platform. In examining the Bible narrative, it is right that we should eliminate from our mind a good deal that is of the nature merely of human interpretation of the divinely-vouched record of this epoch-making event.

In the first place, we dare not ignore the statements of Scripture concerning *the supernatural forces* which God employed in launching the great Flood so that it was not a mere chance combination of natural and presently observable processes. In fact, Scripture presents the Flood as a unique, once-for-all, never-to-be-repeated event of earth history, comparable in magnitude and significance only to the final judgment of the world (Gen. 8:21-9:17; Matt. 24:37-42; and II Peter 3:5-7).

Second, and even more serious, some scientists and theologians "wilfully forget" (II Peter 3:5-7) that God is not only living and personal, but is completely capable of accomplishing exactly the kinds of miracles attested to in His Word. In fact, the Bible is emphatically clear that no one can be a true Christian apart from an acceptance of such stupendous miracles as the bodily resurrection of Jesus Christ from the grave on the third day following His crucifixion (Rom. 10:9; I Cor. 15:1-10).

One hundred and twenty years before the Flood came, God revealed to one human being His purpose to destroy the earth by water and instructed him to make preparation for this judgment by building an ark that would be the instrument for saving not only his family but also the seed of all air-breathing creatures in the world. This structure was significant   not only for its spatial dimensions and proportions, but also in its time dimension; for the hundred years of its construction provided a visible demonstration of God's unwillingness that any man should perish and served as an open invitation to salvation from impending doom.

In the Scripture history two immediate causes are assigned for the Deluge, viz., an excessive rainfall, causing an extraordinary rising of the rivers and lakes, accompanied by a subsidence of the land below the sea-level, allowing the ocean to submerge it ; for it is stated "that the fountains of the great deep were broken up, and the windows of heaven were opened " (vii. 11).

Let us now inquire what great moral and spiritual lessons are taught us by Mount Ararat.

The first lesson is, that "THE WRATH OF GOD IS REVEALED FROM HEAVEN AGAINST ALL UNGODLINESS AND UNRIGHTEOUSNESS OF MEN." Ararat, with his hoary head and shoulders draped with cloud, stood like a grim old sentry watching the destruction of the world of the ungodly, and he cries aloud to men, that "The soul that sinneth it shall die"; that "The wages of sin is death." At the same time we are reminded that the God of all the earth has "no pleasure in the death of the wicked, but that the wicked turn from his way and live." For the Divine judgment did not fall without warning upon that ancient world, "when once the long-suffering of God waited in the days of Noah while the ark was a-preparing." The Lord gave men space to repent when He said that though his "Spirit should not always strive with man, yet his days should be 120 years"; but they repented not. We also are told to "account that the long-suffering of God is salvation," for He is "long-suffering to usward, not willing that any should perish, but that all should come to repentance." That great mountain surely still testifies to a world that has anew rebelled against Him of the forbearance of God.

But Ararat witnesses to THE MERCY AS WELL AS TO THE FORBEARANCE OF GOD; for "the ark," we are told, "rested upon the mountains of Ararat." It witnesses to the effectiveness of the ark for the purpose for which it was constructed. We may picture to ourselves the strange vessel in process of building, or floating on the waste of waters with its precious freight; but Ararat bids us see it moored in port, its voyage successfully accomplished. Its beams and planks and pitch have kept the billows out. The ark preserved its inmates from a watery tomb, the force of the flood of Divine wrath being restricted to the sprinkling of their floating home with the drenching rain or its immersion in the driving waves—"the like figure whereunto baptism doth also now save us, not the putting away of the filth of the flesh, but the answer of a good conscience toward God by the resurrection of Jesus Christ." Its voyage over, "the ark rested upon the mountains of Ararat"; as Jesus, the true Ark, having accomplished his mission, now rests on the mount of God above. As typified by the ark, Christ is the Saviour of the whole creation, as well as of man its natural head. For as "we know that the whole creation groaneth and travaileth in pain together until now," so we know that the whole creation is represented in the prophetical writings as rejoicing in the completed redemption. Mount Ararat may be viewed as a Titanic tombstone marking the grave of the old world of lust, violence, and crime; but it may be as correctly viewed as the Plymouth Rock of the world in which we dwell, the landing-stage where the vessel was moored which carried the Pilgrim Fathers of the world's early youth into the new world; the new era into which the race of mankind then entered—an era of mercy, an era of grace.

Mount Ararat witnesses to PEACE BETWEEN GOD AND MAN. The dove bearing the olive-leaf plucked off has ever since been the symbol of heavenly peace. Peace is a precious gift from God to man—precious when breathed by Jesus after his resurrection on his assembled disciples; precious when whispered by the Holy Spirit in the secret chambers of the soul; but precious also when its symbol was carried to Noah by the gentle dove. Man had involved the lower creatures in his own ruin; yet these first brought him the news of peace and redemption which they shared with their head.

> Sweet dove, that homeward winging,
>   O'er endless waves thy lonely way,
> Now hither bendst thee bringing
>   The long-sought olive spray;
> It tells that love still reigns above,
>   That God doth not his own forget,
> That mercy's ray upspringing
>   Shall light the lost world yet.
>
> THOMAS MOORE.

Noah's dove bringing the welcome message that there was "peace on earth, good-will to men," was the precursor of the Holy Dove, the sweet messenger of rest, who, winging his way from heaven above, found no resting-place in our sin-deluged earth till He alighted on Jesus, the Church's true Ark, and abode upon Him. And now, "being justified by faith, we have peace with God through our Lord Jesus Christ."

Ararat witnesses also to AN ALTAR (viii. 20). Its stones were taken to build an altar before they were taken to build a house, for God must be first with us. Noah by his example bids us seek first the kingdom of God. The new earth, the earth in which we now dwell, was consecrated by an altar. The same expression is used regarding the acceptableness of this sacrifice to God as was used of the Jewish sacrifices which were offered according to his appointment—" the Lord smelled a sweet savour." It was, however, no Jewish offering, but a Gentile sacrifice ; and the heathen nations retaining sacrifice in their worship probably derived it from this altar of Noah on Ararat ; and the fact that our world was spared so long was owing to that sacrifice, and to the great Lamb of Calvary of which it was the forerunner. Both were sacrifices for the world ; the one offered in its infancy, the other in its age. The fact that the lower animals had been saved along with Noah from the Flood makes apparent the suitableness of their being offered to their Creator and Redeemer. This reminds us how they completed their service and homage to the world's Infant Saviour at his birth :

> Fit watchers they of his rude bed,
> Who their vicarious blood had shed
>   For Him so long,
> While all creation travailèd
>   In pain and wrong :
> Knew they that on the altar-wood
> Of Calvary He should shed his blood
>   For us, for them ;
> And win his creatures' gratitude
>   In one joint hymn ?

The sacrifice on Ararat was likewise typical of that on Calvary, and superior to all the sacrifices of the Mosaic law, because, while its efficacy was not confined to a single nation, it was also perpetual—never being repeated, but extending to all time.

Mount Ararat witnesses to A NEW COVENANT BETWEEN HEAVEN AND EARTH—a covenant of blessing, of which Noah's sacrifice was the sanction, and the rainbow was the sign. For whether or not it was o'er the cliffs of Ararat that the various rainbow hues did first unite, it was there that they first formed "in heaven's sight the arch of peace."

> When o'er the green undeluged earth
>   Heaven's covenant thou didst shine ;
> When came the world's grey fathers forth
>   To watch thy sacred shrine :
>
> And faithful to the sacred page,
>   Heaven still rebuilds thy span,
> Nor lets the type grow pale with age
>   That first spoke peace to man.

The rainbow seems to intimate that this purified earth shall form part of the eternal home of the redeemed sons of Adam. Ararat will be there in the new earth, guarding Armenia as of old, which, so often deluged with the blood of her sons and daughters, shall enjoy enduring peace.

This bow shall be seen again on the mount on which the New Jerusalem is built, encircling the throne of God, "in sight like unto an emerald," catching its prevailing hue from the bright green of a revivified earth ; while we hear the Father's voice comforting his people as of old, " For this is as the waters of Noah unto Me. For as I have sworn that the waters of Noah should no more go over the earth, so have I sworn that I would not be wroth with thee, nor rebuke thee. For the mountains shall depart and the hills be removed ; but my kindness shall not depart from thee, neither shall the covenant of my peace be removed, saith the Lord that hath mercy on thee."

Before you turn the page, let me put to you, my reader, these simple questions :

Have you, "moved with fear," fled from the wrath to come, to Jesus who has been prepared by God to be his people's Ark of safety?

Have you been brought by Jesus through the flood of wrath, and been introduced by Him into a state where old things are passed away, and all things are become new?

Have you welcomed the Divine Spirit as the Heavenly Dove, and received from Him a token of peace?

Have you built an altar to God your Saviour, and have you offered to Him all that He asks you for?

Are you dwelling under the arch of peace, remembering that though its beautiful hues are transient, the new covenant of which it is the divinely-selected token is eternal?

II.

Mount Moriah

The Mountain of Sacrifice.

GENESIS xxii. 2; 2 CHRON. iii. 1.

UNLIKE the majestic mountain-mass of Ararat, MORIAH is a small hill that would attract scant notice in physical geography, but the place which it holds in the history of the Church of God is at least as important as that held by the mountain of the ark. The associations of Ararat were with the world at large; those of Mount Moriah are wholly with the Hebrew race and Jewish Church. Its interest begins in connection with the promise made to Abraham, and ends with the destruction of the Temple which stood upon it. Yet Christianity would be almost an enigma without the light shed upon its doctrines and worship by the story of Mount Moriah.

This hill was in the border between the tribes of Judah and Benjamin, to the east of Mount Zion, from which it was separated by a deep gorge called the Tyropœon, or Valley of the Goldsmiths (or, as others say, of the Cheesemongers). From the Mount of Olives, which rises to the east of it, it is separated by the Valley of Jehoshaphat. In the days of Abraham it was overgrown with dense thickets, while its top presented a bare rock well fitted for a natural altar. Its rocky summit was afterwards levelled by Solomon into a beautiful platform for the Temple; while its crest, called Es-Sakhra, the Rock, remains still in its natural state, a mass of rock sixty feet long by forty feet broad, rising seventeen feet above the pavement, surrounded by a railing and silken canopy in the centre of the Mosque of Omar.

Moriah was just outside the ancient city of the Jebusites ; and in David's days was under cultivation, the rock that crowned it being used as a threshing-floor by Ornan, one of the Jebusite citizens. The hill was afterwards included within the area of Jerusalem as extended by Solomon, who built on it the great sanctuary of the national worship. Solomon also bridged the chasm between it and Mount Zion, on which the royal palace stood, by an arched viaduct, called "The Ascent by which the King went up into the House of the Lord," which caused such astonishment to the Queen of Sheba on the occasion of her visit.

On Mount Moriah, as we behold Abraham standing with uplifted knife over Isaac—the son of his old age— we are taught that WE MUST BE WILLING TO SACRIFICE TO GOD WHATEVER HE CLAIMS FROM US, be it ever so dear. If the Most High calls for your health, your goods, your child, your spouse, your life, surrender these to Him freely, and it becomes a sacrifice well-pleasing to God. The voluntariness of the surrender turns what would else be an inevitable loss into an acceptable offering. But this first sacrifice on Moriah, the most wonderful on record, was an uncompleted sacrifice, and was never intended by God to be completed. Indeed, none of the sacrifices ever offered on Mount Moriah were complete. But this offering, though uncompleted, was not incomplete ; for God regarded it as complete : "Because thou hast done this thing, and hast not withheld thy son, thine only son" (Gen. xxii. 16).

It is the Lord's wont to take the will for the deed. Persons are sometimes prevented from carrying out their purpose of service or sacrifice by some providential barrier, by a closing of the door, by a voice from heaven, by God clearly declining the offer. This was the case again in regard to David's desire to build the Temple on this very site long

after. Twice over, on Mount Moriah, we hear the voice
from heaven saying, " Thou didst well that it was in thine
heart."

The next lesson taught us by Moriah is, that "THE LORD
WILL PROVIDE." The patriarch Abraham considered this
to be the main lesson which the memorable occurrence was
designed to teach, for he named the spot *Jehovah-jireh*, "The
Lord will provide"; and the name " Moriah " given to the
hill, evidently after this incident, has the same significance.
In the course of the narrative the promise is thrice repeated.
It is a promise which is full of comfort to God's people
in all seasons of stress and want. The time when our cove-
nant-keeping God, who cares for us, will make the provision
is not indicated, nor the method ; but—

> In some way or other the Lord will provide !
> It may not be *my* way, it may not be *thy* way,
> But yet in *his own* way the Lord will provide.

While this name of Moriah bids us cast all our care upon
Him who careth for us, we must remember that its original
reference was to the provision of the sacrificial lamb—Abraham's lamb then, God's Lamb in the fulness of time. We
learn here that it is only "with Christ" that God also freely
gives us all things. He who provided a Lamb for the
world in the Person of his own Son, will not withhold from
us any good thing. The sacrifice on Moriah was unique ;
for while other sacrifices are provided by the worshipper,
apart from any consent on the part of the offered victim,
here we have brought into prominence the willingness of
Isaac, then in the fulness of his youthful strength, to allow
himself to be bound upon the altar ; and we have in Abraham
a type of the Eternal Father, and are taught that the sacrifice
of Calvary proved the love of the Father as fully as the love
of the Son. It is a living picture of the words : " For God so
loved the world that He gave his only-begotten Son." The
sacrifice on Moriah teaches us, more plainly than any other

recorded sacrifice, THE GREAT DOCTRINE OF "SUBSTITU-
TION." Abraham, we are told, "went and took the ram,
and offered him up for a burnt-offering in the stead of his
son." It was a vicarious offering; and in its relation to
Isaac it becomes a telling type of the Lamb of God, who,
with his sacred head wreathed and caught in the thorns of
a fallen world's curse, died "the Just for the unjust."

We are told also in the New Testament that THE GREAT
DOCTRINE OF THE RESURRECTION was taught on Mount
Moriah. "By faith he that had received the promises
offered up his only-begotten son, accounting that God was
able to raise him up even from the dead, from whence also
he received him in a figure" (Heb. xi. 17–19). It was
under this great strain on his faith, obedience, and affection, that man first grasped the glorious consolation of
the resurrection of the dead.

Passing from Abraham to David, we find another
impressive scene transacted upon Mount Moriah. It was
here that at the command of God the angel who had
slain by pestilence 70,000 men of Israel because of their
monarch's sin, stayed his hand that held the drawn sword
stretched out over the devoted city of Jerusalem. In
2 Chron. iii. 1, this striking incident, which took place at the
threshing-floor of Araunah, the Jebusite, is assigned defi-
nitely to Mount Moriah, the site which David selected for
the erection of the Temple which was built by his son
Solomon. The great lesson of this scene is that NATIONS
UNDER GOD'S MORAL GOVERNMENT SUFFER FOR THE SINS
OF THEIR RULERS. If this was so in ancient times, when
the people were only indirectly responsible for their rulers'
conduct, the righteousness of the Divine action is much
clearer to-day, when in the foremost nations the choice
of the rulers and the decision on matters of public policy
are entrusted to the suffrages of the people. Rulers and
subjects form one body politic with national duties and

responsibilities, the failure to discharge which calls down Divine judgments.

It was the self-moved mercy of God that prompted Him to say to his angel, "It is enough; stay now thine hand": but it was only after sacrifice had been offered and accepted that the angel put up again his drawn sword into its sheath.

That the site of the altar of the temple was bought from a heathen who offered it without price, along with his oxen for the sacrifice, the threshing-instruments for wood, and the wheat of the floor for the meat-offering—is surely suggestive of the bringing of all the Gentiles within the covenant of grace; and that the God of Israel is really their God, whom they will yet freely acknowledge and worship. This Jebusite farmer gives us a beautiful example of how our homesteads, and the scenes and implements of our ordinary labour, should be consecrated to the Lord; while David's reply, "Nay; but I will buy it for the full price: for I will not take that which is thine for the Lord, nor offer burnt-offerings without cost"—is surely a stinging rebuke to many who are only too eager to do this very thing.

From this occurrence Mount Moriah became the site of the Jewish temple. "Then David said, This is the house of the Lord God, and this is the altar of the burnt-offering for Israel" (1 Chron. xxii. 1). It has been said that Moriah seems to have been formed for sacrificial worship, with its rocky plateau partially isolated from what was to be the site of the Jewish metropolis, which it adjoined; while it is itself overlooked by the Mount of Olives, where the crowds of worshippers could view the priests engaged in presenting the appointed offerings. It was the Hill of God to which during the whole period of the subsistence of the Jewish Theocracy the tribes went up to the testimony of Israel.

The arcana of Israel's worship were all preserved here.

The presence of Jehovah, their God, was manifested here during many centuries in the Shechinah cloud of glory. But at last Ezekiel saw it retiring from the temple by slow stages to the Mount of Olives; and after the restoration of the exiles from Babylon, it never reappeared. The sacrifices continued; but the Lord withdrew the sacred symbol of his presence because of the confirmed rebelliousness of his people. For—

> Not all the blood of beasts,
>   On Jewish altars slain,
> Could give the guilty conscience peace,
>   Or wash away the stain;
> But Christ, the heavenly Lamb,
>   Takes all our sins away—
> A sacrifice of nobler name,
>   And richer blood than they.

This thought carries us down to the time when "the Lord, whom his people sought, suddenly came to his temple." On this Moriah, within its sacred shrine, Jesus was presented in infancy to the Lord God. Here as a boy of twelve He was found listening to the Rabbis, and asking them questions; here as a man He taught the people. From the hill-top opposite He foretold the destruction of the temple on Moriah; but in his doctrine He taught them that his own body was the true Temple in which the Divine presence dwelt, and that if that were destroyed He would build another. And as the temples of Solomon, and Ezra, and Herod were now superseded by the Temple of his body, so this fleshly Temple was to be succeeded by a spiritual house in which the Divine Spirit would reside, and where all those who worshipped the Father should worship Him in spirit and in truth, presenting to Him spiritual sacrifices acceptable to God by Jesus Christ. He who had thus come to his own house was at once priest, altar, sacrifice, and temple, all in one. These were the shadows of which the body is Christ. On Himself, as the true Moriah, the

Rock of Ages, the new Church which He founded was to be built. No doubt in this new Church still visible there has been, and still is, much that is transient—much that must be shaken, that the things that cannot be shaken may remain. But if there is much that is imperfect, and therefore transitory, in all forms of Church government, and worship, and life, there is more that is abiding. The presence of God will abide ; Christ will be with his people alway, even to the end of the world ; the Holy Spirit will abide in them, and dwell in them ; the Christian Church will abide, for against it the gates of hell and the grave shall never prevail ; and the Word of God, "which liveth and abideth for ever," will be their unshaken, though not unassailed, charter and infallible guide.

This "mountain of the house" to-day has become, as was foretold, as "the high places of the forest" (Micah iii. 12)—*i.e.*, the site of a false worship. The Mosque of Omar desecrates the ground where the holy and beautiful house stood so long. Its pleasant things are all laid waste, and of its structure not one stone is left upon another. He who has provided the Lamb for the great Sacrifice has provided simple and spiritual ordinances of worship, suited to nurture reverence, piety, and faith in the hearts of the worshippers. And it becomes us to see that we who truly worship in the great spiritual Temple of Christ's mystical Body, adhere to the divinely-appointed ordinances of worship, and do not revert to the ritual and ceremonies of a dispensation that has vanished through age, as it was foretold that it should.

Still less dare we adopt those rites, ceremonies, or doctrines of heathenism which in the early portion of the dark ages were engrafted on Christian worship, and are still retained in some of the corrupt branches of the Christian Church, and whose votaries are putting forth new efforts to have their use extended. If the Lord finally withdrew his presence from a Church which had been so privileged and so dear to Him, and left her house desolate, notwithstanding that all its ordinances and appointments were of his own institution, can we imagine that He will favour with his abiding presence Churches which of their own motion resuscitate a system which He had doomed to perish, and revive puerile and hurtful forms of will-worship which never had the Divine approval, but against which even the Levitical worship was a standing protest? Our Churches cannot do better than study the important lessons taught us by Mount Moriah. But we as individuals must learn these lessons too; and in order to impress them let me, before bidding Moriah farewell, ask my readers:

Have you learned that the Lord will provide? and that not only in the great crises and necessities, but in the little incidents and wants of life? and that it is in and with Christ that He who spared not his own Son will freely give you all things?

Do you know that God so loved the world that He gave his only begotten Son to be the sinner's Sacrifice and Substitute? that Christ took our place upon the altar, and suffered in our room and stead? that the Father had his share in this sacrifice in providing the Substitute, and the Son in willingly giving Himself up for us all?

Have you learned that all other sacrifices and offerings were of worth only as preparatory types of this great offering, or as sequences of it, and derive all their value from the precious blood of Christ?

III

The Mount of Mizpah

The Mount of
Witness and Watching.

GENESIS xxxi. 44–49.

THE Mount, or Mound, of MIZPAH differs from all other hills that will engage our attention in this volume, in its being an artificial mound rather than a natural hill. The artificial mound, or cairn, however, with its pillar attached, was raised upon Mount Gilead, which was one of the summits of the long range of the mountains of Gilead which lie east of the Jordan valley, in the territory afterwards assigned to the tribe of Gad, forming the boundary between Palestine and the regions belonging to the races that had the seat of their dominion in the plain of Mesopotamia.

This extensive range, which presents to the eye an unbroken mountain-barrier on the eastern border of Palestine, is cleft by three deep defiles, through which the streams of the Jarmuk, the Jabbok, and the Arnon, pour their waters into the river Jordan. From the top of the range, looking eastward, we are told that the eye descries "a wide table-land tossed about in wild confusion of undulating downs, clothed with rich grass, and with magnificent forests of sycamore, beech, terebinth, ever-green oak, and enormous fig-trees. These elevated downs melt away eastwards into the vast red plain, which, by a gradual descent, joins the Assyrian desert." It was the natural frontier of Israel, and afterwards produced such striking characters in the Hebrew State and Church as Jepthah and Elijah.

The summit usually identified with this Mount Gilead is that now called Jebel Jilad. The prophet Hosea, who is said to have been buried here, refers to it frequently, and ranks this hill along with Tabor, as forming apparently two prominent landmarks respectively on the east and west of Jordan. The name Mizpah, or Watch-tower, while derived originally from the incident which is now to engage our attention, was descriptive of the hill from which there is a very extensive prospect.

When Laban overtook the fugitive Jacob and his company at this point, after their angry controversy, which ended in a mutual covenant of peace, at the instance of Jacob they gathered stones together, and formed a heap, or cairn, near which rose the monolith which Jacob set up for a pillar. This heap, or cairn, was called by Jacob by the Hebrew name of Galeed, or Heap of Witness; while Laban gave it an Aramaic name of the same significance (Jegar-Sahadutha); and they called it also, by mutual consent, Mizpah—Laban saying, "The Lord watch between me and thee when we are absent one from another."

This cairn and pillar formed one of the milestones of Jacob's life. And it is well that we should erect milestones to measure our life's journey. The monumental mound had two aspects—a retrospective and a prospective. It is as important that we should sometimes take A RETROSPECT OF OUR PAST LIFE, as that we should take a prospective view of our future. Memory, with her grave features and thoughtful mien, is as good a guide as hope, with her sunny smile and buoyant step. No doubt memory is not perfect. We cannot remember all our past; and to be able to do so would not benefit us. But we can recall more of our past than we can foresee of our future; and some of our surest prognostications of our future are drawn from our recollections.

From this milestone in his journey, Jacob's thoughts, we

are told, reverted to a former waymark in his pilgrimage. His God had sent his thoughts backward, by saying to him in a dream, "I am the God of Bethel, where thou anointedst the pillar, and where thou vowedst a vow unto Me." That had been indeed a notable night in his history, and experience took the materials supplied by memory, and from them framed a chart for his future march in life. His diary became his guide-book.

A dream is fleeting, and its impressions fading; but a dream of an open heaven over us, with a ladder reaching up to it from the very spot where we are, God standing above it, and bright angels coming and going, is surely a revelation that should abide with us, and never fade till we ourselves have ascended the ladder and reached the heavenly home. That night-dream on his solitary couch did more for the young emigrant than any day-dreams his fancy might draw. He forgot the hard stones on which he had laid his wearied head, when he found that God had pillowed him on kindness; and the dark expanse of the surrounding night became to him as the curtains of Divine love. He forgot that he was a homeless wayfarer, when he viewed the stars as shining bolts rivetting his heavenly Father's roof over his head. He had been given in his dream no wings, whether of dove or eagle, that he might fly upward, and be at rest in the repose of the mansions of the blest; but he had seen a wondrous ladder reaching all the way, which he must climb with firm foot and resolute will.

The ladders which men's own efforts, or fancies, frame to gain the heavenly height are all too short. Some of them do not reach to heaven, and others do not touch the earth; but this holy ladder represented the Son of Man resting on the earth in his humanity, and resting in heaven in his Divinity. The Daysman and Mediator this, between the man who lies in his weakness at the ladder's foot and the eternal God who appears at the top. Jacob began at once the long and arduous climb, his foot upheld from slipping and his heart from fainting by Him who is at once the Way and the Guide to the Father. At the end of his pilgrimage he reached the top; but all along that mysterious ascent from earth and sin by grace to holiness and glory, the angels of God were passing and re-passing upon it with supplies of cheer and succour: for "are they not all ministering spirits sent forth to minister for them who shall be heirs of salvation?"

Can we, too, not remember how some lonely spot became to us the house of God and the gate of heaven? If so, surely every place of our sojourn since then should also be to us a Bethel, of which we can say, "Surely, God is in this place!" From this milestone and watch-tower of Pisgah memory also recalled to Jacob how the Lord had fulfilled his prayer, and had been with him, and had kept him in the way he went, and had given him bread to eat and raiment to put on, so that he was now returning to his father's house in peace. His highest expectations had been more than realized, his most aspiring wishes more than gratified; and now Jehovah, according to his solemn vow, was indeed his God. And yet his father's God and his own God, who had fed him all his life long, and by his Angel had delivered him from all evil, was now exposing him anew to anxiety and danger; but his history teaches us that it is well to wait and see *the end* of the Lord, for if we know not now what He does, we shall know hereafter.

The Mount of Pisgah at least witnessed that his God had been true to him up till now. His stone pillar was a true Ebenezer, bearing the legend, "HITHERTO HATH THE LORD HELPED ME." This second milestone on his life-journey testified that the Divine benediction had by heavenly alchemy transmuted dross into gold, and that when his grasping relative and master "thought evil against him, God meant it for good." We, too, should learn from this Mount, with its " Heap of Witness," that

> Ill that Thou blessest is most good,
> And unblest good is ill.

These qualities are not inherent in events or objects, but in the God who makes disappointments, injuries, sickness, and sorrows, to be channels of rich blessing to those who receive them in a humble, patient, and trustful spirit.

The immediate cause of Laban's pursuit of his fugitive son-in-law was that he missed his household images, and attached the blame of their theft to Jacob or some of his family. The very reason why God called Abraham to leave his ancestral home in Mesopotamia was that he might worship the God of heaven in a spiritual manner uncontaminated by the image-worship which was practised there. Such a materialising worship was altogether unworthy of Him who is a Spirit, and who desires to be worshipped only in spirit and in truth. So important was this in God's sight, that, in order to attain it, the chosen seed had to be separated from their kindred. Of course the pure heathen worship of the Canaanite nations was much more gross, and all intermarriage with them was forbidden. Yet we find that Rachel had stolen her father's images on quitting her country. Thus Mizpah witnesses to the DIFFICULTY OF ERADICATING THE LEAVEN OF UNSPIRITUAL WORSHIP; and the history of the Christian Church proves how apt it is to return, and sadly to deteriorate Churches that were once pure.

From the passages of his life that have come down to us, we know something of the character of Laban's home-idols. Laban certainly made idols of wealth and worldly prosperity. Jacob himself had been far from free from this idolatry. The Star that long afterwards rose out of Jacob testified that MEN CANNOT SERVE GOD AND MAMMON; and while

Jacob was finally purified from Mammon-worship, a long course of very trying discipline was needed to purge his character from it.

Both these patriarchs also MADE AN IDOL OF WORLDLY ASTUTENESS, and did not hesitate to do evil to obtain a temporal good. Jacob's long exile in Padan-aram was brought upon himself by his fraudulent dealings regarding his brother Esau's birthright; and he sorely suffered for this in his later life also, for God often allows "his own iniquities to take the wicked himself."

> He made a pit; he digg'd it deep;
>   He digg'd it for his brother;
> But for his sin he did fall in
>   The pit he digg'd for t'other.

Both these men MADE AN IDOL OF SELF. Each of them loved himself, and sought to aggrandise himself at the expense of his brother. Jacob had been slowly weaned from self-love, but Laban was still worshipping at the shrine of self; for Jacob, indignantly charging him with having in his own interest changed his wages ten times, asserted that except the God of Abraham and the Fear of Isaac had been with him, he would surely now have sent him away empty. A remarkable change, amounting practically to what we term CONVERSION, was wrought on both their characters on the Mount of Gilead. In Jacob's case it was completed a day or two later, at his next resting-place of Peniel, when at last he yielded entirely to God, and finally renounced his own method of saving himself, as, sensible of his own weakness, he halted on his thigh, after his mysterious wrestling with his nameless antagonist, till daybreak. He then received the new name of Israel, in recognition that he was now a prince with God. We have no record of the further spiritual history of Laban, but considering that it was he who took the leading part in explaining the full significance of the name they together gave to the Mount, and that he parted from Jacob in fast friendship which he never violated, we may surely conclude that a similar change was wrought in him. Jacob, when he discovered that these idols were really in his household, shortly afterwards insisted that they should put away all their strange gods, and with his own hands "he hid them under the oak which was by Shechem."

But how many persons still sacrifice their honour, probity, happiness, even their hope for eternity, at the altar of self, which is the cruellest, and most insatiable of all the idols that rob God of his due worship, and men also of what is their due.

The Mount of Mizpah now witnessed to A MUTUAL COVENANT THAT NEITHER WOULD HENCEFORTH INJURE THE OTHER. Laban said to Jacob, "This Heap be witness, and this Pillar be witness, that I will not pass over this heap to thee, and that thou shalt not pass over this heap and this pillar to me, for harm" (ver. 52)—a covenant of amity which they loyally observed. But should such a covenant be an unusual occurrence? Are we not all bound by such obligations, not only towards special persons, but towards all our fellow-men?

Yet does not history record the miseries that have arisen in the world through the breach of such obligations? Do not our newspapers witness to the neglect by nations of this message from Mizpah? Do not our family annals show how it has been disregarded in that sphere? And do not many blighted and saddened lives testify that it is little obeyed between man and man? Have not our Churches sorely suffered from the breach of such a brotherly covenant? Whether they can now attain close union or not, is it not incumbent on them to cultivate warm unity of spirit, and to take their great Feast of Friendship, which, alas, has become the monument of their strife, as a witness that none will pass over it to the other for harm?

Is not such a hostile passage a trampling on the broken body of their Redeemer?

The second table of the law is briefly comprehended in the beautiful saying of our Lord, "Thou shalt love thy neighbour as thyself." He has shown us, moreover, that we are to recognise as our neighbour all whom we encounter in life's highway, whether travelling, or lying fallen by the wayside. He also extends the obligation from the negative one of refraining from injuring our neighbour to the positive one of rendering to him, in the spirit of the Good Samaritan, all the succour that we can, even at much inconvenience, and, it may be, loss or jeopardy to ourselves.

It were well for us all often to visit this Mount of Gilead, to study its testimony, and to learn therefrom that "LOVE WORKETH NO ILL TO HIS NEIGHBOUR," and is the fulfilling of the law, to strive to do good unto all men as we have opportunity, and to love our neighbour as ourselves.

The Mount of Mizpah also displays the beautiful legend, "THE LORD WATCH BETWEEN ME AND THEE WHEN WE ARE ABSENT ONE FROM ANOTHER!" The monogram of Mizpah is sometimes engraved upon bracelet or locket, and there is no more fitting device to maintain in the memory friendship, fidelity, and mutual love. The word is itself a jewel and a charm, in the light of its significance and origin. What a happy talisman for separated friends to bear about with them!

The Lord God is here recognised as having a place in the group, and that not the last place—but the first. He comes before self, and before our neighbour, as He ought to do. If we set God first, all our other relationships will fall into their right order. The Lord is willing to join the company of all those who are willing to enjoy his society, and to invite his presence; for it is not unduly extending the words of Jesus to apply to all such his comforting assurance: "Where two or three are gathered together in

my name, there am I in the midst of them." Our natural
relationships ought to be sanctified by grace, which elevates,
beautifies, and perpetuates them by projecting them into
eternity.

The Lord is not only the bond uniting together every
little group, or larger company of his people, but He links
together those who are far separated. Members of a
family become scattered to distant continents ; intimate and
loved friends become severed by wide oceans—but how sweet
to know that if they are Christ's they are still closely united.
We may be absent from one another, but are never absent
from Him who gave us as his farewell : " Lo, I am with you
alway, even unto the end of the world." Jesus is nearer to
us than our next of kin ; than our most tenderly loved ones ;
than those who are ever by our side. He will never prove
a wedge to sunder us, but a golden band to bind us closer ;
and his presence and uniting influence are not impaired by
any interval of space or time. If Christ is nearer you than
the friend nearest you, and nearer your brother in Africa or
China than the friend nearest him, then you and your brother
can hardly be said to be absent from one another. Not
only may you be united in thought, spirit, and affection,
but you are each looking into that loving eye that is watching over both. In that eye of infinite tenderness you might
each almost behold the reflected features of the other.

But this "absence one from another" includes the
absence caused by death and the grave. The spirit that is
absent from the body seems to nature to be removed from
us by awful distance ; almost infinite remoteness from
all earth's interests and love seems inscribed on the face of
the departed, even

> Before decay's effacing fingers
> Have marr'd the lines where beauty lingers.

But those who sleep in Jesus when absent from the body
are present with the Lord ; and as the Lord is always

present with his saints on earth, these lost ones, too, are not far from them. We cannot hold communication with them, and have no Scripture warrant to pray for them. How could we pray aright for those of whose wants we are utterly ignorant? And would it not be a reflection on their Lord's love to them, and distrust of his tender care of them, to intercede on their behalf with Him who will anticipate all their requirements long before our tardy prayer could reach Him, even if we knew what they might require? To those who ask whether there is any statement to this effect in Scripture, we may reply in the Saviour's own words : " If it were not so, I would have told you." If He said that He was going to prepare a place for them before their arrival, that surely implies that He will not neglect providing amply for them in that place when they have reached it. In bidding, then, a last farewell to a dear one going home, the mourner may comfort his heart by this old-time assurance, " The Lord will watch between me and thee when we are absent one from another."

May we not extend this Mizpah aspiration to our relation to our absent Redeemer Himself? He assured his sorrowing disciples, " If I go away, I will come again." Regarding Him who, in his humanity, became our next of kin, our Elder Brother—yea, the loving Bridegroom of the company of his people, which forms the mystical bride, the Lamb's wife, may we not use reverently this olden petition, " The Lord watch between me and thee when we are absent one from another "? Such a prayer binds us to remember Him, and to act as his representatives on earth, as we know that He remembers us, and acts as our Representative in heaven.

The scene on Mizpah closes with a solemn breaking of bread together, that seems like an anticipation of a sacramental feast. " Jacob offered sacrifice upon the mount, and called his brethren to eat bread." Whatever character we assign to this meal, it was sanctified by sacrifice and solemn covenanting in the presence of Him who is called the God of Abraham and the Fear of Isaac. It is instructive to observe that the sacrifice was only offered after each had resolutely put away all thought of revenge and all resentment, and had become fully reconciled to his offending and offended brother.

How beautifully in their practice these two patriarchs acted, not only up to the spirit, but to the letter, of the commandment given ages after by Jacob's divine descendant: " Therefore, if thou bring thy gift to the altar, and there rememberest that thy brother hath ought against thee— leave there thy gift before the altar, and go thy way; first be reconciled to thy brother, and then come and offer thy gift." If this watchtower of Mizpah teaches us these lessons, the cairn and the pillar on the top of Mount Gilead will not have been erected in vain.

As we pass on from this mount, let me ask: Do you sometimes take a retrospect of the way you have been led in your past life ?

Are you prepared to renounce heart-idols, that you may render to God an undivided service ?

Are you earnestly seeking to exercise that love which worketh no ill to one's neighbour ?

Are you willing to forego revenge, and to forget injuries done to you ? Do you remember that being reconciled to your brother is the necessary prelude of all acceptable worship ?

Are your heart and way such that you can ask the Lord to watch you with His pure eye ?

IV

𝔐𝔬𝔲𝔫𝔱 𝔖𝔦𝔫𝔞𝔦

The Mountain of
the Law.

EXODUS xix. 20.

SINAI, one of the most famous mountains in Scripture history, stands near the southern end of the Arabian peninsula, where it projects between the Gulfs of Suez and Akaba, the two forks of the Red Sea. While there is no dispute that Sinai was one of those stupendous and awe-inspiring granite mountains that are grouped here in a great cluster, separated from one another by steep and narrow valleys, there is not such unanimity as to the individual mountain to which this name should be assigned. Mount Serbal, which was early adopted as Sinai, apparently from its imposing character, must be rejected on account of its having five striking peaks instead of one. On the whole there seems little doubt that the true Sinai is the mountain which still bears that name, and which has been compared to a gigantic cathedral separated by narrow lanes from lofty houses on either side. This comparison is the more natural, since the whole group of the Sinaitic mountains has been called "a city of almighty masonry"—the bare rock ridges, running now in parallel rows, now at all manner of angles, being like piles of gigantic buildings, the dividing gorges (or Wadys) being the intervening streets.

This oblong mass is three miles in length, with its true summit at the southern end still bearing the name of the " Mount of Moses " (Jebel Mousa), and overlooking a plain (Wady Sebayeh) amply sufficient to contain the vast camp of Israel. The northern peak of this same block, however (Sasâfeh), has many who support its claim to be the true Sinai, and it also towers over a plain (Er Raheh) which is large enough for Israel's encampment. The face of this latter summit towards the plain is marked by precipitous cliffs. This fact rather supports the claim of the Mount of Moses to be the true mountain where the Law was given, inasmuch as the direct ascent of Sinai from the camp is stated in the sacred narrative to have been barred, not by natural precipices, but by bounds set by Moses at the command of Jehovah. Whichever summit is selected, the general impression made by the surroundings is the same.

Travellers tell us that "a scene more solemn than that before Sinai cannot be conceived. The desert wanderers were led through a city of rock more awful to men from crowded Egypt than the most gorgeous capital to men from a solitude. In the heart of that 'city' they passed before one mighty monument of the power of its Builder. There He manifested Himself, and from its towers He uttered the Law 'with a great voice' which swept the plain, and made the multitude cry out, 'Let not God speak with us lest we die!'"

Rising from the vast tracts of Arabia, it became the ascent by which our race was led up to meet and hold intercourse with the Glorious One who inhabits Eternity ; for here He descended to commune with his creatures. In Egypt they had dwelt on a low level morally and spiritually ; here they were raised to a lofty platform, though only for a brief season—yet some few among them continued to walk with God in these heavenly places. Men have often selected lofty mountains whereon to study the laws of nature. In our own land Schiehallion was chosen to test the law of gravitation, and Ben Nevis to exhibit the laws of winds and storms. Sinai was divinely selected that men might there receive the knowledge of the laws of God's moral government, including mercy as well as righteousness and judgment. What was there presented to the ear and the eye of the Israelites and their leaders were the shadows of heavenly things rather than the substance thereof; yet we must remember that most of our astronomical knowledge has been gained by a study of the shadows and reflections of the heavenly bodies, rather than by a direct inspection of their substance. The knowledge may be imperfect, but it is not misleading because derived from " shadows."

All nations of the world to which the Word of God has come have been impressed by Sinai and its revelation, and have with one consent adopted its legislation as the foundation of their laws.

What are the main lessons in the moral law which Mount Sinai with its thunders has pealed in the ears of men from the days of Moses till our own time?

The first of these is that since Sinai with its revelation succeeds the revelations of Ararat and Moriah, THE LAW IS IN EVERY SENSE POSTERIOR TO THE GOSPEL, with its salvation by faith preached from the stranded ark, and to the inculcation of substitution and sacrifice on Moriah. The Apostle argues, " This I say, that the covenant (of promise) which was confirmed before of God in Christ, the Law which was 430 years after cannot disannul, that it should make the promise of none effect " (Gal. iii. 17). The Gospel was no afterthought to make up for the deficiency of the Law—it was the Divine plan for the bestowal of eternal life from the beginning, and the Law was added to be " our schoolmaster to bring us to Christ," whose office was foreshadowed in the ark and the altar, which had been revealed on earlier mountains. The Gospel is no innovation, but is the original and enduring purpose and plan of salvation for our sin-ruined race.

On Sinai we are taught that LAW IMPLIES A LAWGIVER;

that moral law implies a moral Lawgiver. The preface to
the Law is, "I am Jehovah thy God!" The proclamation
of the law opens with a declaration of the existence of God,
and the unity of God. In this it offers a contrast to the
religious system of Confucius, which, with much truth in it,
has proved a failure, apparently because it left unsettled the
great question of the existence of God. How clear the message, "Hear, O Israel, the Lord our God is ONE LORD!"
"Thou shalt have no other gods before Me!" (*Commandment* i.).

We are next told that the worship which we are to render
to God must be rational, moral, and spiritual in character,
because God is an intelligent, moral, and spiritual Being.
All worship, therefore, of a sensuous character is forbidden,
such as that by images or pictures (*Com.* ii.). Our worship
is to be reverent, and not a worship of empty form, but
practical, else it is "in vain," a thing of emptiness and
nothingness (*Com.* iii.). Does this not describe a great
deal of what passes for worship? True religion is intended
to benefit the body as well as the spirit; and one of the
great blessings it secures for us is *rest*—rest for the body for
its own sake, as well as a type and pledge of rest for man's
burdened spirit. This 4th Commandment is classed as
one of our duties to God; but it is rather given in the form
of a privilege for ourselves, which it is our duty to secure
also for our neighbours—a duty never more clamant than
at the present day. Our servants as well as ourselves have
a right to this rest; it must be secured even for the dumb
animals that toil for us. This rest is given in a charter
from the Great Creator. Human life, in its derivation, its
continuance, and its transmission, is to be held in honour
and preserved inviolate by us (*Coms.* v., vi., vii.). All such
heathen customs as exposure of aged parents to die, suicide,
suttee, infanticide, legalised impurity, are to be put down by
the civil magistrate. Private property is to be protected by

him (*Com.* viii.), as modern legislation protects it against all forms of theft, embezzlement, fraud, and oppression of the weaker classes of the community. On Commandment ix. rests our whole actions at law for libel, slander, etc., which have assumed such prominence in modern jurisprudence.

Under all these laws the crimes are classed under a head drawn from a flagrant case (murder, adultery, theft, etc.). In *Com.* x. it is the *root* and not the *fruit* of the sin that is struck at in its heart-searching prohibition, "Thou shalt not covet." This teaches us that the Divine law reaches to the inmost thought as well as to its outcome in word and deed. No statute of any State legislates for thought as does God's statute-book. Paul states that it was by the 10th Commandment that he was convinced that he was a law-breaker; and it has had the same effect on many others.

On Sinai we are taught that THE MORAL LAW IS A REVELATION, and not an evolution. No doubt the great principles of the law here engraved on tables of stone had from his creation been inscribed on the fleshy tablets of man's heart. Paul asserts that the heathen "show the work of the law written on their hearts; their conscience also bearing witness." But when that inscription had by The Fall been sadly defaced, a new and fuller copy was given us by the same Supreme Lawgiver. These laws, then, were not the result of centuries of legislation, but were revealed from above. They were promulgated by prophetic authority, though enforced by that of the magistrate. In their grand principles they are obligatory on all men in all ages. Christ's exposition of the spirituality of this Law, and his extension of its scope, merely show that it was inherently perfect, although the apprehension and application of it in the age of its first publication were imperfect.

A Scotch theologian has said that the impossibility of attaining to a perfectly sinless conformity to this high standard, was a pillow of thorns to the believer, while it was a couch of down to the hypocrite. In my late father's diary I find the entry, " If there is anything I can affirm without hesitation or abatement, it is 'Oh, how I love thy Law!'" and every true believer would at least desire to say the same.

Sinai also teaches us that THE SERVICE WHICH OUR GOD ASKS FROM US IS A FREE SERVICE, not a bond-service. The preface to the Law is, " I am the Lord thy God which have brought thee out of the house of bondage." The true and only sufficient motive to induce and enable us to keep the Law, is gratitude to Him for redemption. Even on Sinai the Gospel is proclaimed before the Law. Gratitude to God is called for in the preface, and love to Him in the very heart of the Law (*Com.* ii.). The Divine mercy is thus exhibited in the very forefront of the Decalogue, in which the Lawgiver proclaims, " Mercy unto thousands of them that love Me and keep my commandments." So also the name of Jehovah was published on Mount Sinai in answer to his servant's prayer, "I beseech Thee show me thy glory!" as "the LORD, the LORD God, merciful and gracious, . . . forgiving iniquity, transgression, and sin." It is God's glory that " mercy rejoices against judgment." One would naturally say that this will make him who breaks it careless about the Law. On the contrary, there is forgiveness with Him in order that He may be feared.

The whole ceremonial Law given on Sinai was a revelation of mercy, a dispensation of grace, a system of pardon and cleansing. The Tables of the Law were placed in the Ark of the Covenant beneath the mercy-seat, the blood-drops sprinkled upon which covered the transgressions of the law-breakers. The moral law was a fence within which the fruits of righteousness grew and matured under the shining of God's lovingkindness and the fertilizing dews of the Holy Spirit.

The moral and ceremonial Laws of Sinai formed a

Covenant of Grace, and not a new covenant of works; but it was a preparatory and imperfect covenant of grace. Here we see a revelation of the inherent holiness of God, and of the righteousness which He demands of men, and also of his mercy which unites these two, and bestows on us that which He requires from us. In both its branches the Law was given not to bestow life, but to bring us to Christ, that we might be justified by faith. The moral law-giver drives men to Christ by his rod, closing every other door to eternal life and blessedness; the ceremonial law-giver points men to Christ through pictures, models, and signs, which, very imperfect in themselves, yet throw a clear light, as object lessons, on the perfect Saviour.

> This cloud-wrapt hill attend thou still,
>   And him that went within,
> Who yet shall bring some worthy thing
>   For waiting souls to see—
> Some sacred word that he hath heard,
>   Their life and light to be.

Let me ask you, my reader, whether you are convinced that without holiness, without obedience to the moral law, no man shall see the Lord? Have you also learned that your best obedience is so imperfect that you cannot obtain eternal life in this way, and that you must obtain it as a free gift, through the Gospel proclaimed long before the Law was given, through Jesus, the true Ark, and the true Substitute and Sacrifice; not by your own merits, but through that mercy which is enshrined in the very forefront and heart of the ten commandments? Has the law been your schoolmaster to bring you to Christ?

V

The Rock in Horeb

"That Rock was
Christ."

EXODUS xvii. 1–7; NUMB. xx. 7–13.

THIS mountain-rock has a peculiar interest for God's people in every age. It is interpreted by St. Paul to have been A VISIBLE SYMBOL OF CHRIST: "That Rock was Christ"; and among all the Old Testament types of Christ it is the only one that is known to be still extant. This does not, however, imply that we can with absolute certainty point to it and say, "This rock is the ancient type of Christ." We know that it was in Mount Horeb, which was adjacent to Mount Sinai, and which was probably the name of the mountain block of which the Mount of Moses is the southern summit. Rephidim, where the Israelite camp was pitched, was one day's journey north of Sinai, apparently in the broad valley, now called the Wady-es-Sheikh.

When the people murmured here for water, Moses was called to go up into Mount Horeb, along with the Elders, where he met God on the top of the chosen rock. The monks of the Greek convent near Sinai point out a large mass of red granite with marks on it, apparently caused by running water, as the rock which was smitten by Moses. It lies at the foot of a lofty precipice (on the west side of the Mount of Moses), from which it has evidently fallen, the precipice itself having a broad vertical channel on its face, such as would be caused by water flowing down. No water flows there now, but there is water at the base of the rock. Whether this cliff in the narrow gorge of the Ledja be the true rock or not, the self-same rock that was struck by Moses must stand as of old somewhere in this neighbourhood. Water springing from such a rock would naturally flow down into the Wady-es-Rahah and the Wady-es-Sheikh (where in the rainy season a torrent still takes this course), on to Rephidim, where the great camp was.

Another noteworthy peculiarity of this Smitten Rock is that it was really A TYPE IN DUPLICATE. At the end of their forty-years' sojourn in the wilderness, the Israelites again suffered from want of water in Kadesh-Barnea, on the very borders of the Promised Land. The site of this second rock has been much debated, but there seems reason to identify it with a bare mass of rock standing at the north-eastern corner of a plain shut in by mountains, which is named " Ain-el-Kadeis," the Fountain of Kadesh. At the foot of this rock a copiously-flowing spring bursts forth, falling in beautiful cascades into the bed of a torrent, and after a course of 400 yards, loses itself in the sand. This site, first discovered by Rowlands and Williams in 1842, is accepted by Dr. Thomson and other competent judges as correct. Of it Dr. Andrew Bonar writes, " That well began to flow on the day when Moses and Aaron struck the rock twice, and it has ever since flowed on."

In regard to the rock in Horeb, and its stream, there is no indication whatever in the sacred narrative that the miracle was continued during the forty-years' desert sojourn. When Paul, therefore, says that " they drank of that spiritual Rock which followed them," he either refers to Christ Himself being in the midst of Israel through the whole desert sojourn, as the people's spiritual sustenance and refreshment; or if he calls the drink furnished by the Rock "spiritual" because it was supernaturally given, he indicates that the stream accompanied the camp in its divinely chosen movements. Or it may be that other rocks yielding water were found by the pilgrim Church wherever they pitched, maintaining in the ordinary course of Providence supplies which were miraculously inaugurated and closed at the two Meribahs.

Each of these rocks is small compared with many of the hills of Scripture. This spiritual Rock does not bulk largely in the eye of the world, as Ararat and Sinai do, but it bulks large in the eyes of God's people, though it is a rock rather than an Alp. If you ask why the people of God form such a high estimate of it, our answer is, Because " that Rock was Christ." Let us enquire how this Rock resembles Jesus Christ, and what lessons regarding Him it teaches to the intelligent beholder.

Its want of imposing grandeur to the eye taught the Israelites that their Messiah when He came should not appear to be different from other men. As this rock was formed of material like the surrounding rocks, so Christ's body was formed of the dust of the ground, like our own. " He was made in the likeness of sinful flesh." More than once He escaped violence simply by being lost in the crowd. Though He was, to the eye of faith, " the chiefest among ten thousand and altogether lovely," yet He was despised and rejected of men.

> The Saviour came ; no outward pomp
> Bespoke his presence nigh,
> No earthly beauty shined in Him
> To draw the carnal eye.

Some persons acknowledge that the world sorely needs renovating and reviving spiritual influences from above, such as might be presented under the figure of life-giving rain descending from the clouds of heaven; but they refuse to receive such influences when offered to them through the channel of the human nature of Him whom his people accept as the world's Redeemer. No doubt his human nature was derived (though without taint of sin) from our own, but it became the wondrous receptacle of that Divine

Spirit which proceeds from the Father and the Son, and became the channel through which alone his spiritual influences can be communicated to men. To such objectors "the Rock of Ages" is but a "rock of offence," but the man who is deeply sensible of his own need will thankfully use the words of Psalm cxiv. ; and as he quaffs the living and life-giving stream of grace, will praise Him,

> Who by his power did turn the flint
> Into a water-spring.

This Rock WAS DISTINGUISHED FROM OTHER ROCKS BY THE PRESENCE OF JEHOVAH upon it—no doubt, in the pillar of cloud : " Behold, I will stand before thee there upon the rock in Horeb" (Ex. xvii. 6). So the Baptist was told that he would recognise the Messiah by a similar sign : " Upon whom thou shalt see the Spirit descending and remaining on Him, the same is He which baptizeth with the Holy Ghost." Jesus said of Himself, " The Spirit of the Lord God is upon Me." Very probably the symbol of Jehovah's presence on this rock was not visible to all the people whose encampment was miles away ; but it was so to Moses. The Shechinah cloud of glory may have been hid from their view among the other clouds that robed the mountain. As John alone saw the dove lighting on Jesus, and Moses alone may have seen this cloud, so his countrymen perceived no special Divine presence in Christ. The eye requires to be divinely opened to behold the divinely manifested presence.

This Rock had a HIDDEN STORE OF PRECIOUS WATER WITHIN IT, visible only to the eye of the All-seeing. Its fountain of springing water represented the Holy Spirit, of which Jesus said, " If any man thirst, let him come unto Me and drink. But this spake He of the Spirit which they that believe on Him should receive, for the Holy Ghost was not yet given, because that Jesus was not yet glorified " (John vii. 37). Under the symbol of pure water bursting forth from a rocky fountain, the Holy Ghost is represented as the source at once of life and satisfaction to men perishing from the unquenched thirst of their immortal spirits for that which no stream of earthly satisfaction could ever supply.

For when the Christ of God came into our world men were dying, craving for the eternal satisfaction which they could not find in any earthly cisterns. All other religions had failed to give to men the true knowledge of God; governments had failed to repress sin and crime; civilization had failed to elevate; art had failed to give appreciation for the highest beauty; arms had failed to give man the conquest over himself; luxury had failed to appease his cravings; philosophies had failed to discover the true wisdom. Then in man's extremity came God's opportunity. Christ came, and gave the promise of the Holy Spirit which dwelt in Him without measure. But it was only after He was smitten by the rod of the lawgiver, and died under the stroke, that the living water poured forth. The water flowing from his pierced side is as well attested as the Blood. Both are of equal and of inestimable importance.

The condemnation and execution of the Lord of Glory were the work of the law on One "who died for sins, but not his own." The priests and the populace, Pilate and Herod, were but the unwitting rod grasped in the hand of the lawgiver. It was really under the stroke of justice that Christ "was once offered to bear the sins of many." Now Moses' sin consisted not only in his angry retort to the rebel people, marring the meekness in which he excelled; not only in his unbelief, trusting to the efficacy of his rod rather than to the promise of his God (and faith is not perfected till it can discount and discard the use of means from its calculation)—but very specially in his smiting the rock on the second occasion at all, when he had been

commanded only to speak to it. By doing so *he spoiled
one of the most instructive types of the Saviour's death.*
For Christ was not to die twice ; but "as it is appointed
unto man once to die, so Christ was once offered."
The offering of Christ again by Romish priests in the
Sacrifice of the Mass is a most pernicious error ; and
had Moses' second striking of the rock (viz., in Kadesh)
been allowed to pass uncensured and unpunished, good
ground would have been given for that Popish dogma.

It would have seemed to teach that He could be slain more
than once, and therefore that the atonement which He offered
on Calvary was incomplete, for if the worshippers had "once
been purged there would have remained no more offering for
sin." But now "by one offering He hath perfected for ever
them that are sanctified." After Christ's death all that is
required of those who are seeking the gift of the Holy Spirit
is that they should "speak to the Rock, and it shall give
forth its water"—*i.e.*, should pray to the living and glorified
Saviour, and He will give us that Spirit who came down on
the Church at Pentecost after his crucifixion, of whom He
said, "If I depart I will send Him unto you." If the stream
which flows now from the rock in Kadesh is the very stream
which first sprang forth under Moses' rod, it teaches us that
the Holy Spirit is still proceeding from the ascended Christ
in as great fulness as ever, to satisfy the thirst of every one
who will come to the living Rock of Ages and drink therefrom. However this be, the invitation is still given : "The
Spirit and the Bride say, Come ; and let him that is athirst
come ; and whosoever will, let him take the water of life
freely."

Both of these rocks were named Massah and Meribah
(Meribah in Rephidim and Meribah-Kadesh), because there
the Israelites tempted God, and strove with Him, saying,
"Is the Lord among us or not?" Moses in his song
relates how Israel "lightly esteemed the Rock of his

salvation," and charges him with being "unmindful of the Rock that begat him," showing that he understood the rock to typify a Person, as did Isaiah when he foretold that "a man shall be as an hiding-place from the wind, and a covert from the tempest, as rivers of waters in a dry place, and as the shadow of a great rock in a weary land." He indicates that under this great rock they were sheltered from the storms that raged around, and that here also they were shaded from the hot Arabian sun, as they drank of the fountain which Moses had unsealed. While Moses describes the rock as Divine, Isaiah sings of it as human, which tallies exactly with Paul's statement, "that Rock was Christ."

While Christ still, as of old, is a stone of stumbling and a rock of offence to multitudes, who provoke the Lord to anger by their unbelief, we must remember that here also the Lord's ambassadors did not display the meekness and gentleness of Christ in commending Him to a rebellious people, and for this error were excluded from the earthly Canaan. Is there not here a lesson for Christ's servants— whether ministers, evangelists, or Sabbath-school teachers— when, provoked by the opposition of those whom they seek to instruct and benefit, they "preach Christ of strife and contention," rather than "of good-will," and in the spirit of the Master, and so may themselves be chastened for offering Christ to the perishing in a spirit that is not Christ-like? But Christ Himself gives to the rebellious these gifts which He had specially received of the Father for them, that God the Lord may dwell among them.

May every weary wanderer in the wilderness of life say, in the words of Dr. Horatius Bonar:

> Oppress'd by noonday's scorching heat,
>   To yonder Rock I flee ;
> Beneath its shelter take my seat—
>   No shade like this for me.

> Beneath that Rock clear waters burst,
>   A fountain sparkling free ;
> And there I quench my desert thirst—
>   No spring like this for me.

Yea, may he learn to say with Toplady :

> Rock of Ages, cleft for me,
> Let me hide myself in Thee !

In closing this short study of the Smitten Rock, let me ask :

Are you, my reader, convinced that you must perish unless you receive the gift of the Holy Spirit, who alone can satisfy, by his presence and influence, the cravings of your immortal spirit ?

Have you learned that the Holy Spirit is given and received only through the death of the Redeemer, who was stricken and smitten by Divine justice because He bore our sins ?

Have you come to this smitten Rock of Ages ? And as a thirsty one have you drunk of the life-giving fountain to which all may repair without a price ?

VI

Mount Hor

The Grave of Aaron.

NUMBERS xx. 23–29.

MOUNT HOR is situated in Arabia Petraea, not far from the rock-hewn Edomite capital of Petra, and rises 5,300 feet above sea-level, being 1,000 feet higher than our highest Scottish mountain. It has two peaks, on the western and higher of which stands a mosque, built over the reputed tomb of Aaron, the first Jewish high priest. From the summit of Mount Hor all view of the Land of Promise was shut out by an intervening mountain barrier, while the prospect that meets the eye presents

> A billowy ocean of mountains hoary,
>   A chaos of cliffs round this awful spot ;
> Splintered, and blasted, and thunder-smitten,
>   Not a smile above, nor a hope below,
> Shivered, and scorched, and hunger-bitten—
>   Horror and ruin, and death and woe.
>
> H. BONAR.

The summit of the mountain where the high priest died is composed of white chalk, resting upon new red sandstone, which is pierced by "dikes" of red granite and porphyry. Deep red and pure white, overhung by the blue heaven and pierced by the golden sunbeams, met Aaron's gaze as he climbed this mountain. Red, white, blue, and gold, surrounded him in his death, as they had done in his life's ministry in the tabernacle. Well versed as he was in the reading of such symbols, he must have been impressed as he ascended from the red, emblematic of the sacrificial blood, to the white, of pardon and purity ; while overhead was the constant infinite blue of the heaven he was about to enter, and the golden glory with which he was so soon to be clothed. This forms the ascent of every child of God to heaven, and the order is always the same.

This majestic mountain is the grandest sepulchral monument containing the honoured dust of a great man, through the night of time till the morning of the Resurrection. Three Hebrew children, who played in company together in the hut of Amram, and who afterwards influenced the world's legislative and religious history more than any other family has done, had often gazed in wonder in the plains of Egypt, at the massive sepulchres of the Pharaohs; but—

> No pyramid tomb with its costly grandeur
> Can once be compared with this mountain shrine;
> No monarch of Memphis is swathed in splendour,
> Great priest of the desert, like this of thine.

Precious in the sight of the Lord is the death of his saints; and He assigns to this spiritual prince of his people a more than princely burial. The snow-white chalk of the peak of Hor was a glorious winding sheet, doubly significant as it wrapped the honoured dead reposing on the blood-red rock.

From the situation of the tomb chosen by his God we may infer that AARON OFTEN COURTED SOLITUDE, AND CLIMBED A MOUNTAIN APART TO PRAY. It is not uncommon for persons to indicate the locality where they would desire to be buried. This was very marked in the case of the Hebrew patriarchs. Jacob and Joseph both charged their families to lay their remains in the land which the Lord had promised should be the possession of their descendants. We may feel sure that Jehovah, in choosing a lonely mountain as the burial-place of Aaron, gratified a deep wish of his servant's heart. For most of his life Aaron's home had been in the rich delta plain of Egypt, and for the last forty years he had dwelt in the desert plains of Arabia, yet often in vales in the immediate vicinity of rugged and rocky mountains. In these flat plains, with the Egyptian or Arabian sun flooding each rood of ground with its glaring rays, there was little opportunity for the retirement which he needed and loved ; so he must have sought it in the mountains at the base of which Israel's tents were pitched. He loved to be alone with God. His character was not so rock-like and self-contained as that of his brother Moses ; he was not so well-fitted to stand alone against a multitude. Still, probably the very sense of his deficiency in this respect drove him to seek for strength in solitary communion with his God.

Aaron was not afraid to meet with God alone. Once a year he went alone into the presence of Jehovah in the inner sanctuary ; but far oftener he, in solitude as deep and still, sought audience of Him who dwelleth not in temples made with hands, and held communion with his Maker, within nature's veil of cloud and among the mysteries of creation, where, as well as in the Holy of Holies, the Divine Shechinah dwelt. He withdrew into the recesses of Nature, where the angels prepared the manna, and where at the rising and setting of the sun his faith might see each bush still glowing with the light of the Divine presence.

If Jesus followed any example among his predecessors when He went out into a solitary place, or up to a mountain to pray, as He so often did, it was surely that of Aaron, whose priesthood He came to assume to Himself. Aaron did not shrink from being alone in his grave, because he had been used to be alone with God in his life, and found it good to be in this sacred solitude, where he had trained himself in the spiritual worship of the Unseen, by withdrawing even from those sensible symbols allowed under the Old Testament economy.

It was meet that Aaron should be honoured with a more than regal tomb, because HE WAS A VERY HUMBLE SAINT. It has ever been God's way to bestow grace and honour

upon the lowly.   In the families of the Hebrew patriarchs
the elder had never, until we come to Aaron, been willing
to yield the first place to the younger brother.   Ishmael
mocked Isaac because he was the heir of the promise ;
Esau sought to slay Jacob because he obtained the blessing ;
Joseph's elder brothers envied and hated him because his
father loved him.   Of Aaron it is said that he was "glad in
his heart," when he met his younger brother Moses returning from his long exile to be the leader of his people.

He gladly took the second place, although he had many
qualifications for the first.   His training under the eyes
of his godly parents, instead of at the court of Pharaoh ;
his freedom from the impulsive spirit of Moses ; his greater
knowledge of his countrymen, and his natural gift of
eloquence—all fitted him to be leader.   But God dwells
with the lowly spirit, and he chose Aaron, not to be the
ruler of the nation, but as the man who was to dwell in his
courts.   His family occupied the highest offices of the
sanctuary for 1,500 years, while the family of Moses sank at
once into obscurity.   Such honour was allotted to this saint
because of his humility.   On the occasions on which he
failed in this grace, he was clearly led away by the hotter
spirit of his sister Miriam, or by the people.

We see the humility of this disinterested man in holding
up his brother's hands on Horeb.   He was willing all
through life to be the mouthpiece of Moses, and to receive
the Divine revelation wholly from him.   It was trying for
him when the formula in Exod. vi. 26, "these are that
Aaron and Moses," was changed in the next sentence to
"these are that Moses and Aaron," never again to be
written in the order of primogeniture.   Even when mur-
murers arose against his holding the highest sacerdotal
office, he left the vindication of his position to Moses ;
while at his brother's bidding this noble man ran with the
fire from the altar in his censer, in his eagerness to make

atonement for those who had so wronged him. It was then that his cut rod was made to bud and yield almonds, as a lasting memorial of his right to his high position.

This saintly man was characterized by UNMURMURING SUBMISSION AND UNQUESTIONING OBEDIENCE TO THE DIVINE WILL. He who presided over the offering of the sacrifices had learned to sacrifice his own will. When his two eldest sons Nadab and Abihu died for offering strange fire before the Lord, their father "held his peace." That silence is more impressive than all his eloquence. It was surely a sacrifice of himself offered with hallowed fire.

He also did God's will by daily performing ordinances that must have appeared mysterious to him. Aaron was the first man called to obey the ceremonial law, which was, according to St. Peter, an intolerable yoke, and which must have appeared to some extent unmeaning. For this law did not appeal to the conscience, like the moral law. Moreover, it had not been revealed to him, but he received it from his brother. He delighted to do God's will whenever it was made known to him. He no doubt failed at Meribah-Kadesh in obedience, as also did Moses, when they struck the rock; as he had failed at Sinai, when at the instigation of the people he made the golden calf; but these exceptions proved that obedience was the rule of his conduct.

Aaron was THE TYPICAL SAINT OF OLD TESTAMENT TIMES. He is called "the saint of the Lord" (Psa. cvi. 16). He was called with a holy calling; he washed often at the laver; he offered acceptable sacrifices to God. He had free access to God, and could "approach the mercy-seat." He dwelt in the courts of the Lord; he pondered much on the mysteries committed to his charge, which were full of Christ, and thus would grow in knowledge and grace and in bringing forth the fruits of the Spirit. He was the great precursor of all believers, enjoying in type what they now enjoy in fulness. If we realize our position as priests to

God, we are merely coming up to the ideal which was pre-
figured in Aaron.

Aaron, also, both in his office and his character, TYPIFIED
THE LORD JESUS. Like Jesus, he was meek and lowly in
heart; like Jesus, he learned obedience, and learned to say,
"Thy will be done!" Like Jesus, he had "compassion on
the ignorant, and on them that were out of the way"; like
Jesus, he made atonement, and also made intercession for
others. His prayers were very prevailing. He was brought
into contact with the sins of men. In a sense he bore the
sins, and represented the persons of sinners, bearing on his
heart the names of the people of God. While tender
towards the erring, he was "faithful to Him that appointed
him." He sprinkled on transgressors the cleansing blood
and the water of purification. He forgot self, and lived for
others. He learned much of redemption among the shadows,
and then went up to see and enjoy its substance. "Seeing
then that we have a great High Priest that is passed into
the heavens, Jesus the Son of God, let us hold fast our pro-
fession, and let us come boldly to the throne of grace," as
Aaron did, "that we may obtain mercy, and find grace to
help in time of need!"

At the close of his life Aaron calmly submitted while
Moses disrobed him, and arrayed his son in his priestly
garments, and so demitted his priestly office to his successor.
Then the tabernacle of his body was taken down, soon to
be dissolved in dust, just as the Tabernacle in which he
ministered so faithfully was to pass away, as its curtains
and bolts and pins had indicated. The dispensation which
he inaugurated was to be removed, "that the things which
could not be shaken might remain." This priest was "not
suffered to continue by reason of death," while his great
Successor "hath an unchangeable priesthood, because He
continueth ever."

And then it is said, "AARON WAS GATHERED TO HIS

PEOPLE." His remains were laid beside no kindred dust, therefore this beautiful expression indicates that his immortal spirit was gathered to the spirits of just men made perfect. His fathers by faith gave commandment concerning their bones, and were laid in their last resting-place in the Cave of Machpelah; but Aaron, in a still stronger faith, gave no commandment concerning his bones. He was willing to be buried in a lonely grave on a mountain-top, with no view of the Land of Promise to gladden his closing eyes ; with no green turf to be his coverlet, telling of life even on the tomb. "I am going to be among my own people," were among the last words I heard from an honoured Christian Scottish lady. And such was the epitaph written over the first Jewish High Priest, giving a home-like aspect even to such a solitary tomb, and telling us that the emancipated spirit had entered the many-mansioned House above.

> Alone and safe in the holy keeping
>   Of Him who holdeth the grave's cold key,
> They have laid thee down for the blessèd sleeping,
>   The quiet rest which his dear ones see.
> While the breeze bears the sound of a nation weeping :—
>   Oh, who would not rest by the side of thee ?
>
> H. BONAR.

Let me ask the reader to apply to himself the lessons taught by the death of Aaron on Mount Hor, and to inquire :

Do I take opportunities for private devotion ; and do I seek from time to time to be alone with God ?

Do I know something of Aaron's humble spirit ; and am I willing to yield to others the first place ?

Have I learned to submit my will to the will of God ?

As Aaron was divested of the priestly office before entering God's presence, where he stood in need of the priesthood of another, so am I sensible that I also need the sole mediation of Jesus Christ the Great High Priest, who is passed into the heavens ?

VII.

Mount Pisgah

The Hill of the Goodly Prospect.

DEUT. xxxii. 49, 50.

PISGAH is the name of a summit in the range of Abarim, in the land of Moab, which has not been identified. It appears to have formed part of Mount Nebo. Canon Tristram has described a panoramic view which he got from one of the peaks of this range, which was about the height of Ben Nevis, 4,500 feet, three miles south-west of Heshbon, which he conjectured might be Pisgah. The prospect, which is very like that which met the eyes of the aged leader of Israel's tribes as they were about to close on this world, he describes thus :

> To the north and east were the hills of Gilead, and the vast expanse of the goodly Belka, one waving ocean of corn and grass. Southward appeared Mounts Hor and Seir, with other granite peaks of Arabia. Turning westward, there lay before them the Dead Sea, the whole valley of the Jordan, and all the familiar points in the neighbourhood of Jerusalem. North of the capital their eyes rested on the rounded top of Gerizim ; and further off there opened up the Plain of Esdraelon, a shoulder of Carmel, showing to the right of Gerizim, while the faint and distant bluish haze beyond it told them that there was the "Utmost Sea." It seemed as if but a whiff were needed to have brushed off the haze, and revealed the Mediterranean clearly. Northward still rose the unmistakeable Tabor, aided by which they could identify Gilboa and Little Hermon. Snowy Hermon's top was mantled with cloud, Lebanon's range being shut out from view exactly behind it.

This would imply (if this peak were Pisgah) that Hermon was taken by Moses as representing Lebanon, of which it is really the loftiest summit. This magnificent panorama realizes the view that was presented to the undimmed eye of Israel's aged lawgiver, and shows that the representation given of the extensive prospect was no fanciful picture.

Some very important lessons are taught to every reader of the narrative of Moses' death and burial on this mountain of the Goodly Prospect.

We learn that THE DAY OF DEATH IS FIXED BY THE DIVINE DECREE, and is not dependent on sickness, or accident, or old age. These, which are certainly factors in determining the length of our life, are to be accounted as the instruments for carrying out the Divine purpose. Although disease is often overcome by the physician's skill, and accident averted by prudence, the ultimate determinant of each life is the Will of God. The prophet's "eye was not dim, nor his natural force abated," when the Lord spake unto Moses, saying, "Get thee up into Mount Abarim, unto Mount Nebo, and behold the land of Canaan which I give unto the children of Israel, and die in the Mount." This mountain guards the grave of a great man who died not from natural causes, but simply at the bidding of the Lord. But do any die otherwise than at the mandate of the Lord, who recalls when He wills the spirit which He gave? The departure of one of Moses' greatest successors is described in the words, "When the Lord would take up Elijah into heaven by a whirlwind. . . ." So, whatever be the immediate cause of the death of any of God's children, the proper way of recording it, and that which alone can console the mourners is, "When the Lord willed to take my father, my husband, my brother, my child, up into heaven by a consumption, a fever, a shipwreck, or a bullet, the Lord sent him to such a place to meet the chariot, with its burning steeds and wheels, stationed to part the loving and loved ones asunder, and bear one of them to glory." The recognition of this great fact should not make us neglect the use of means for prolonging life, but it should lead us to use prayer to the

God of our life as the chief of all those means. And when the means fail, it should lead us calmly to submit to the unerring appointment of Him "who has appointed to man his bounds that he cannot pass," and to say, "The Lord gave, and the Lord hath taken away; blessed be the name of the Lord."

We are taught here not only that "there is no man that hath power over the spirit to retain the spirit" in the day of death, but that the death of the child of God should be AN ACT OF VOLUNTARY SELF-SACRIFICE, even as the death of Moses, and of the Greater Prophet than Moses, was. Men should not meet death as their fate, or their doom, but should be ready to render up their life as the last act of obedience which, in this world, they can offer to God. Our Lord has left us an example of being "obedient unto death," which it behoves us to follow. This aspect of the death of the believer is well expressed in the words of the old hymn :

> The hour of my departure's come ;
> I hear the voice that calls me home :
> I come, I come, at thy command ;
> I give my spirit to thy hand.

Another lesson taught us on Mount Pisgah is that "THE WAGES OF SIN IS DEATH." The Lord said to his servant, "Die in the Mount . . . because ye trespassed against Me at the waters of Meribah." Pisgah is a monument reared by the Builder of the eternal hills to testify that even a single sin has for its due wages, death ; and that sin in the Lord's people is not less hateful to God than sin in those who are impenitent and unpardoned. In some respects it is more hateful ; for it is in evidence where it is altogether out of place, where it would not have been looked for, and where, unless in mercy covered, forgiven, and forgotten, it must constantly meet the eye of the Holy One in a way that the sins of the unpardoned do not confront Him. From these

He that is of purer eyes than to behold iniquity can hide his face by turning away from the sinner himself, while that pure eye, that is ever upon the righteous, must be offended by the constant sight of his people's sins.

Moses' death outside the Promised Land also warns us not to imagine that our virtues and victories over sin will compensate for our failures and falls. "The man Moses was very meek above all the men which were upon the face of the earth"; but on account of failing once through lack of this grace, when he cried with Aaron, "Hear now, ye rebels; must we fetch you water out of this rock?" he was visited with signal punishment. When his faith in the Almighty failed on this occasion, when "he believed not God, to sanctify Him in the eyes of the children of Israel," his meekness failed also. If the root-grace of faith fail, then will all the virtues quickly wither.

From Moses' dying without being permitted to enter the Promised Land, we conclude that ALL PERSONS DO NOT DIE ETERNALLY WHO DIE FROM THE CONSEQUENCES OF THEIR SIN, AND UNDER DIVINE JUDGMENT. Moses' death was a visitation in judgment of his transgression, and he died under the same doom as the whole congregation of Israel, "whose carcases fell in the wilderness." Yet we find him at a later period talking with the Greater Prophet on one of those very hills which he had viewed from Pisgah's summit, and which he had longed to be permitted to tread.

He conversed with Jesus on the Mount of Transfiguration "regarding the decease (which, translated exactly, is The Exodus) which He was about to accomplish at Jerusalem" a far greater exodus this, from the dominion of sin and the grave, than that which he himself led out of Egypt. We are warranted, therefore, in concluding that many of those who died in the wilderness for their sins, like their leader only "seemed to come short" of the rest and the inheritance; and that many whose lives since then have been similarly cut short by their sins, have yet not failed by God's grace to attain "the rest that remaineth for the people of God." A man may die because of his sin, and as the result of it, without dying *in* his sins. We are therefore warranted in pressing, with all earnestness and hopefulness, eternal life on those whose days on earth are sadly shortened by the sinful courses they have followed.

When death carried off Moses, HIS LIFE-WORK WAS COMPLETED. This great man could say, as few can, "Exegi;"—"I have finished the work which Thou gavest me to do." He calmly set in order all that he had been concerned with, knowing that the time had come for him to die. This arranging of his affairs in prospect of his death is more marked in the case of Moses than any other Bible saint, except the Son of Man. The whole book of Deuteronomy consists of a series of addresses spoken in preparation for his decease. Death did not overtake him unready. He renewed the national covenant, rehearsed God's dealings with the people, reviewed his life, re-edited the law, supplied omissions, wrote up arrears, pronounced blessings, and rounded off his life-work. Then he rested from his labours, and his works have followed him ever since. Being dead, he yet speaks to all generations of mankind. His laws have moulded the legislation of all Christendom, and of all the Mohammedan races. No epitaph is inscribed over his unknown grave; but his own writings are his epitaph—that wonderful Pentateuch in which he has withdrawn the veil from the dawn of history, from the very origin of all things, and from their consummation in the first and second Advents of Him who said, "He wrote of Me." He has left us a lesson to have our life-work ready to be closed, and its records made up for the great inspection of posterity and of eternity.

By the death of Moses on Pisgah we are taught that THE LAW MADE NOTHING PERFECT. Such perfecting is

assigned to Him who has brought in "the better hope";
for this man, whose life strikes us as so complete, did, after
all, not quite complete his mission. Jehovah " brought his
people out that He might bring them in "; but He brought
them out of Egypt by Moses, and brought them into
Canaan by Joshua. And as his mission was uncompleted,
so the long-cherished desire of his heart was ungranted.
"I pray Thee," he had cried, " let me go over and see the
good land that is beyond Jordan!" But the Lord would
not hear him, and said, " Let it suffice thee! Speak no
more to Me of this matter!" (Deut. iii. 23–26).

So the world's great reformers, Statesmen or Churchmen,
have often died without seeing the fulfilment of that for
which they had long and earnestly toiled. Moses died
under a law that seems almost as fixed as his own moral
laws, that the man whose task it has been to labour for, and
secure the introduction of, a new era, dies before that
era dawns upon his country or his Church. Moses died,
not having received the promise, but having seen it and
embraced it. It is Jesus who leads his people into the
rest that remaineth, as by the ministry of his namesake,
Joshua, He led Israel after Moses' death into the land of
earthly rest. We are told that "what the Law could not
do, in that it was weak through the flesh, God, sending his
own Son," did. It is the Gospel and its heralds, and not the
Law and its ministers, that can alone lead sinners into the
inheritance of the saints. The magistrate administering
the law, as Moses' successor, may secure the well-being of
the State ; but it is the minister of the Gospel, ordained
by its great Author, whose honourable place it is to lead the
sinner condemned by the law, and harassed by an accusing
conscience, into a true rest, and into the inheriting of the
goodness which God has "prepared for the poor."

The grave on Mount Pisgah proclaims that THE LORD'S
PEOPLE ARE STRANGERS AND PILGRIMS ON THIS EARTH.

This stranger in Midian for forty years, a wanderer in the desert for forty years more, and at last buried in foreign soil, declared plainly that here he had no abiding city, but sought one that was to come. His history has stamped the earthly life of the people of God as a pilgrimage. The most commanding personality in all history, he was unostentatious in his life, simple in his diet, and far removed from desiring to enrich himself at the expense of the citizens of the commonwealth of Israel. He did not seek ease or self-indulgence of any kind, even in old age, as many do. How often do good men when they grow old relapse into the worldliness which in their best days they renounced !

It was not, the Apostle declares, for want of opportunity that Moses having forsaken Egypt never returned thither even in passing desire. If he assigns their "not being mindful of the country from whence they came out," because they did not return to it, as supporting his statement that the numerous seed of Abraham who died in the wilderness, as a rule, "all died in faith," how much more was it true of their grand old leader ! He assuredly died in faith as he had lived by faith, pressing on to the city whose Builder and Maker is God.

On Mount Pisgah MOSES DIED ALONE, UNTENDED BY KINSMAN OR FRIEND. Such kindly attentions are soothing, and human nature craves them ; but after all, however we may be accompanied to the brink of the dark river, in our passage through it we must be alone—alone, and yet not alone, because the Father is with us. "Though I walk through the valley of the shadow of death, I will fear no evil, for Thou art with me." At several of the most crucial crises of his life the grandeur of Moses' character stands out in its loneliness, but never more so than in his dying, with none near him but the Ever-present.

There was no priest with him to minister the offices of religion, nor was the ministry of affection tendered by any relative or attached follower. This man of God with whom the Lord of heaven had held converse, "face to face as a man speaketh unto his friend," who had himself waited by the side of his dying brother on Mount Hor, had none to watch beside him while his own spirit was passing. Yet he could say with a later prophet of Israel, "Whom have I in heaven but Thee? And there is none upon earth whom I desire beside Thee. My flesh and my heart faileth, but God is the strength of my heart and my portion for ever."

Let those who are tempted to murmur because their loved ones have died untended by the ministry, whether of religion or affection, refrain from fretting when they remember how this most honoured man of God was suffered to die quite alone.

And had he not high honour?—the hill-side for a pall,
  To lie in state while angels wait, with stars for tapers tall,
And the dark rock-pines like tossing plumes over his bier to wave,
  And God's own hand in that lonely land to lay him in the grave?
O lonely grave in Moab's land! O dark Beth-peor's hill!
  Speak to those curious hearts of ours, and teach them to be
    still.

MRS. ALEXANDER.

MOSES WAS BURIED IN AN UNMARKED AND UNKNOWN GRAVE. Most men would shrink from such a burial. Some reader of this page may perchance lament because the remains of one dearly loved are lying where the mourner cannot visit the resting-place, to bedew the sod with tears, or erect a monumental stone to mark the sacred spot. Let such complaining be stilled by the reflection that this friend of God was laid in an unknown grave. For him indeed such a burial had no terrors, because death itself came not as a foe, but as a friend, to usher him into the house of many mansions. "He was gathered to his fathers as Aaron his brother was gathered." Both were buried in solitary graves, but their spirits were gathered to the company of the perfected spirits of the just. This phrase used in Scripture of these two eminent saints does not imply that the human spirit, quitting its mortal tenement, returns to God unclothed. A New Testament Apostle, anticipating the hour of his death, writes : " Not for that we would be unclothed, but clothed upon, that mortality might be swallowed up of life."

The beautiful metrical paraphrase of 2 Cor. v. 1–10, used for generations in Scotland in the praises of the sanctuary, thus faithfully presents St. Paul's teaching on this subject :

> An house eternal built by God
>   Shall lodge the holy mind,
> When once those prison-walls have fall'n
>   By which 'tis now confined :
> We know that when the soul unclothed
>   Shall from this body fly,
> 'Twill animate a purer frame
>   With life that cannot die.

It was probably in this " house which is from heaven " that Moses long afterwards appeared on the Mount of Transfiguration. He may, indeed, have been raised out of his grave in Moab's lonely valley, and thus occupy a unique position among the inhabitants of glory, for neither Enoch nor Elijah experienced a resurrection from the dead. It has been thought that this may be pointed to in the statement that " Michael the Archangel disputed with the devil about the body of Moses" (Jude 9). But there is no indication of such an anticipated resurrection in the inspired narrative—and is the supposition at all necessary? Our body at the hour of death is identical with our body at the hour of birth ; not from any identity of the constituent atoms—for science tells us that these are all changed, nay, indeed, have been entirely changed many times in our life—but because our animal soul and higher spirit have been continuously selecting and assimilating suitable materials for their dwelling, drawn from their surroundings on this earth. When these immaterial parts of our composite being

travel into new regions of the universe, is it not reasonable
to suppose that they will continue their natural work of
building up a material " house to lodge the holy mind,"
composed of constituents drawn from the worlds among
which they now move ; thus forming a body which will be
still our own identical body, but capable more fully of
carrying out the mandates of the governing spirit, and of
reflecting more clearly in feature and expression the holy
nature and distinctive character of its purified tenant?

Mount Pisgah is one of those hills which John Bunyan
has named the Delectable Mountains, which Christian pilgrims are privileged to ascend before they cross the river of
death, and enter the country of the Blessed.

The prospect from Pisgah was fair. The late Dr. John
Duncan once said to me that, as he grew old, he liked to
climb hills to gaze upon the landscape, that he might carry
away with him on his departure as true and fair a remembrance of this world into the next as he could, adding,
" For it's a beautiful world, after all." " ' But these Delectable Mountains,' " said the shepherds to Christian and
Hopeful, " ' are Emmanuel's Land, and are within sight of
his city.' So they went forth with them and walked awhile,
and had a pleasant prospect on every side. Then said the
shepherds, ' Let us show to the pilgrims the gate of the
Celestial City, if they have skill to look through our per-
spective glass.' The pilgrims then lovingly accepted the
notion. So they had them up to the top of an high hill
called Clear, and gave them their glass to look through.
Then they saw something like a gate, and also some of the
glory of the place. Then they went away singing." We,
too, may join them in the strain of our own Isaac Watts—

> Fair fields beyond the swelling flood
> Stand dress'd in living green ;
> So to the Jews old Canaan stood
> While Jordan roll'd between.

Could we but stand where Moses stood, ,
　And view the landscape o'er,
Not Jordan's stream, nor Death's cold flood
　Should fright us from the shore.

Let me now affectionately ask you, my reader, Are you prepared to render up your spirit to God who gave it when He may demand such an offering?

Is your life-work in a state fit to leave it when the summons of death may come?

Have you learned that only Jesus with his glorious gospel can introduce you to true rest on earth, and to glory above?

Are you sojourning here as a stranger, looking for the city which has foundations? And are you seeking even on earth to get some glimpses, at least, of that celestial country and its glories?

VIII

𝕮𝖍𝖊 𝕸𝖔𝖚𝖓𝖙 𝖔𝖋 𝕳𝖊𝖇𝖗𝖔𝖓

The Hill of the
Happy Retrospect.

Joshua xiv. 12.

HEBRON, a famous and very ancient city in the southern hill-country of Judah, " built seven years before Zoan in Egypt," in its earlier days bore the name of Mamre, the Hittite ruler who resided there. The Cave of Machpelah, which Abraham purchased from him, is now covered by a mosque in this city which has still a considerable population. In that cave were deposited the remains of Abraham, Isaac, Jacob, and their wives. The city being afterwards captured by the Anakims, under Arba, was called the city of Arba ; but when it was taken by the Israelites they restored its old name of Hebron, which means, a confederacy. Hebron itself lies somewhat in a depression, but stands at an elevation of 4,000 feet above the Dead Sea, which is overlooked by some of the heights surrounding the town. From the references to it in the sacred history, " this mountain " would seem to comprise a considerable stretch of mountainous country, including the city of Debir, previously Kirjath-Sepher, which was captured by Othniel, who, as a reward for this feat of arms, received Caleb's daughter in marriage. The earlier name indicates that these mountaineers were advanced in literary culture ; for it signifies either " scribes' city " or " book town," while the name of Kirjath-Sannah, which it also bore, signifies the " town of instruction." The inscribed tablets recently discovered at Tel-el-Amarna contain letters dated from Lachish, Jerusalem, Gaza, etc., at this early day. The country in its valleys is exceedingly fertile—Eshcol, whence the spies brought back to Moses the samples of huge and luscious fruit, being within fifteen minutes' walk of Hebron.

The town, which now, in memory of its having been the home and burial-place of Abraham, who was called the friend of God, bears from this the name of El-Kahlil, was King David's capital in the earlier years of his reign. But in the days when Israel, under Joshua, first took possession of Canaan, the hill of Hebron is associated with Caleb, the faithful messenger of Moses, the whole-hearted follower of Jehovah, the man of faith and of enterprise; and teaches us several lessons worth remembering.

Caleb was distinguished as being A FAITHFUL FOLLOWER OF GOD IN A FAITHLESS GENERATION. In the prime of his manhood, having been despatched by Moses from Kadesh-Barnea, as one of the twelve spies to explore the land of Canaan, its cities, its inhabitants, its products, on returning to the camp, he, along with Joshua, gave in "the minority report," the terms of which were, "Let us go up at once and possess the land, for we are well able to overcome it." They acknowledged that "the cities were walled and very great," and that the sons of Anak, who inhabited the mountain country of Hebron, were men of gigantic frame, but described the land as fertile, and its fruit amazingly rich and large.

Caleb said, "If the Lord delight in us, He will bring us into this land and will give it us." It was now that he, with his friend and colleague Joshua, narrowly escaped being stoned by the people, being saved only by the sudden appearance of the glory of the Lord before all the Children of Israel. The Lord threatened to smite the whole nation with pestilence, and disinherit them for their unbelief in his power and promise, and their cowardice in preparing to return under a new captain to Egypt, and offered to make of Moses "a greater nation and mightier than they." At the intercession of that wonderful man of God, the Lord put away his wrath and pardoned the people, but declared that all those who had seen his wonderful works in Egypt and in Sinai and who were of full age to understand them, from twenty years and upward, should die in the wilderness, in which they should wander for forty years, "according to the number of the days in which the spies searched the land, each day for a year." The ten spies also who brought up the "evil report of the land died by the plague before the Lord," Joshua and Caleb alone being spared (Num. xiv. 37, 38).

Now what makes Caleb's faithful following of the Lord very remarkable at this crisis, when fear and unbelief swept away the whole people with a resistless current, is the fact that he was of foreign extraction. His father, Jephunneh, was a Kenezite, a descendant of Esau ; so that like Hobab of Midian and Rahab of Jericho, he was chosen from outside the children of the promise ; yet he excelled all the pure-blooded Israelites in faithful adherence to the God of Abraham, being one of those strangers of whom our Lord said, "I have not found so great faith, no, not in Israel."

This mountain was a witness that CALEB VALUED ABOVE ALL ELSE THE PRESENCE OF THE LORD. "If the Lord delight in us," he said, "then He will bring us into this land ; neither fear ye the people of the land, for the Lord is with us." And when, after forty years had elapsed, the tribes of the wandering foot and weary breast had at last crossed into the Promised Land, this noble man expressed his old faith thus : "Now, therefore, give me this mountain (of Hebron) ; if so be the LORD will be with me, then I shall be able to drive out the Anakims, as the LORD said."

This mountain bore THE RECORD OF A SAD DEFEAT of the host of the Lord. It is narrated that when they proposed to go up into the mountain, Moses sought to dissuade them, saying, "It shall not prosper, for the Lord is not among you. But they presumed to go up unto the hill-top. Then the Amalekites came down, and the Canaanites which dwelt in that hill, and smote them, unto Hormah," *i.e.*, utter destruction.

This mountain witnessed the *fear* of the people, when "they lifted up their voice and cried and wept that night." It witnessed also the *unbelief* of the people. The people refused to believe in the promise of Jehovah, while at the same time they yielded ready credence to the report of the spies. Unbelief and credulity are not so opposed as might be imagined. Even to-day many who disbelieve the sacred record yield all too easy credence to the baseless assumptions and theories of those who attack the veracity of the Scripture history. This mountain witnessed also *the presumption of the people*, and the sad disaster which it entailed. Faith will go nowhere without a Divine warrant, but will go anywhere with such a warrant; just as it will venture nowhere without God's presence, but anywhere with that holy safeguard. Presumption disregards both the presence and the promise of God. It associates itself with self-reliance. On this occasion it took a promise—but a promise to which it had no right, because it discarded the condition attached to it. Therefore, multitudes who reached the border of Canaan never entered it. They lived and died *borderers*.

This mountain is consecrated by THE PLEADING AND THE FULFILMENT OF AN OLD PROMISE. Forty years before, on the memorable occasion already described, God had promised to Caleb the land which he had so faithfully reported on. He recalls the occurrence to Joshua thus: "Thou knowest the thing which the Lord said unto Moses, the man of God, concerning me and thee in Kadesh-Barnea: Surely the land whereon thy feet have trodden shall be thine inheritance and thy children's for ever, because thou hast wholly followed the Lord." It is a good thing to have a promise which we are holding fast and pleading. Caleb had kept hold of this promise for forty-five years, and at last it was fulfilled to the very letter. Does this mountain not remind us that we are often too impatient for the fulfilment of promises? The mountain that had been promised did not flee or melt away, and Caleb was as firm as the mountain. He never swerved from his steadfastness, but rather might be pictured as exclaiming :

> This rock shall fly
> From its firm base as soon as I.

God's faithfulness is like the great mountains. Caleb was spared to be one of the two survivors of an ungodly generation, and ended his life in one of the most God-fearing generations of Israel's history. We can hardly doubt that he and Joshua, fine instances of the " survival of the fittest," largely contributed to make it so, perhaps even more than Moses, who was too elevated above the people to influence them so fully. In his old age he did not lament the good old times, for the new time and order to which these now gave place were better than they.

Of every believer who is weary with waiting it will be said at last, as it was of the Lord's chosen people in the furnace of Egypt, "But the time of the promise drew nigh. . . ." "For the mountains shall depart, and the hills be removed, but my kindness shall not depart from thee, neither shall the covenant of my peace be removed, saith the Lord that hath mercy on thee."

Day after day had this man of God kept his grip of the promise, till more than 10,000 days had dawned and died in darkness. Each of these days only brought him a view of desert sands and barren peaks, instead of the green and fruitful hills of Hebron. But at last his eye rested on a vision which had been his day-dream and night-dream all through those years. This vision had tarried, and he had waited for it, and found that in the appointed time it came, and was not too late. So to every waiting one the vision of heaven will come at last to replace the dream of heaven, and the reality will exceed the fancy.

This mountain was A MONUMENT OF ONE WHO BROUGHT FORTH GOOD FRUIT IN OLD AGE. Mount Pisgah, while a monument of God's faithfulness, was also, alas! a monument of the unfaithfulness, on one occasion in his old age, of the most notable man of God the world ever saw—the man with whom his God spoke "face to face." The Hill of Hebron is a monument of a man of God whose path was as the shining light that shineth more and more unto the perfect day; of one whom his Lord kept from falling and preserved faultless unto the end; whose long trying and testing wrought patience, whose patience wrought experience, and whose experience wrought hope that did not make him ashamed. His trial ended in his triumph. In Caleb we see what aged believers may do, because we see what one aged believer did. The enthusiasm, the enterprise and hope of a young Christian are beautiful, but the enthusiasm, the enterprise and hope of an aged believer are even more beautiful and inspiring. Here is an example for the aged to copy. Caleb excelled other saints in his whole-hearted following of his God, and in his holy enterprise and valiant courage. And he exhibits these graces in old age as well as in mid-life, teaching us that aged Christians should be fired with the enthusiasm and boldness which one would look for in younger men. Some persons as they grow old have reason to sigh—

> Tired, tired and spent; the day is almost run,
>   And, oh, so little done!
> Above and far beyond, far out of sight,
>   Height over height,
> I know the distant hills I should have trod,
>   The hills of God,

Lift up their airy peaks, crest over crest,
Where I had pressed
My faltering, weary feet, had strength been given,
And found my heaven !

May such be able, with the aged Caleb, to add—

But strangely now I know that I do stand
Within the Promised Land,

and be filled and fired with his spirit of holy enterprise, as they behold still farther, loftier, fairer hills rising before them, to attain whose heights must be the object of their earnest desire and strenuous endeavour. The mountain, doubtless, is steep, but strength will be given, even to the aged, to ascend it ; the fastnesses seem unscaleable, but there is a pathway of approach which our skilful Guide will point out to us ; they are garrisoned by gigantic and cruel foes—but if the Lord delight in us, and be Himself with us, we are well able to overcome them.

Aged pilgrim, your God is willing to give you back, if not your youth, at least the hopefulness, the holy enterprise, the sacred dream, of your youth. Some heights of attainments you had aimed at in your early Christian course, but failed to achieve, may yet be yours before you leave this world.

Caleb was the oldest man in the Church of God in his day; but in energy, hope, zeal, and enterprise, he was the youngest. And he was spared to attain and possess, in his old age, those heights which in early life he had simply been able to gaze upon, and long to win.

My reader, remember the doom of those who had reached the border of this hill, but who feared to attack it.

Remember the doom of those who went up into this hill presumptuously, without the presence of the Lord of Hosts.

Remember the reward of him who endured to the enu, who received the promise, who still brought forth fruit in old age, who had the happy retrospect of a consistent life, in which he had wholly followed the Lord, and whose name is held in everlasting remembrance.

IX

Mounts Ebal and Gerizim
The Mountains of
The Curse and The Blessing.

JOSHUA viii. 30–34.

E BAL and Gerizim are two mountains situated in the centre of Palestine, on the south and north of a narrow valley in which stood the town of Sychem, or Shechem, now called Nablous (Naples or New-town), above which they rise some 800 feet. The human voice can easily be sent from one hill to the other; and the children of the place, we are told, still amuse themselves by shouting across the valley.

Moses gave very express instructions before his death that great stones should be erected on Mount Ebal, after the tribes got possession of the land, that a copy of the law should be inscribed thereon; and that the curses attached to the breaking of the law should be proclaimed by the Levites with a loud voice from this mountain, while the blessings annexed to its observance should be similarly proclaimed from Mount Gerizim. Are they not, he said, on the other side Jordan, by the way where the sun goeth down? A missionary settled in Nablous, when on a tour among the mountains east of Jordan, observed at sunset the sun actually sink into the cup formed by the convergence of these two hills between which his house lay. The first place of sojourn of Abraham in Canaan had been at the oak trees of Moreh, not far from Shechem. Under one of these oaks it would appear that Jacob buried the idols of his household. The great lawgiver had set before the people A BLESSING AND A CURSE—a blessing, if they obeyed the law ; and a curse, if they were disobedient. These he held forth for their solemn choice.

All through Scripture, and throughout the whole history of God's dealings with men, this blessing and this curse are clearly exhibited ; but on these twin hilltops they were localized, the one over against the other. On Mount Sinai the law had been proclaimed with remarkable clearness ; but on Sinai the blessing attached to obedience was not made so emphatic as it is on Gerizim. When Jesus Christ gave the law with new authority in his Sermon on the Mount, He specially emphasized the blessings connected with it in the Beatitudes which He pronounced at the very opening of his discourse. Here, then, we have on these twin hills a testimony to the coming Gospel era as an era of blessing.

These hills also witness to THE PERMANENT OBLIGATION OF THE MORAL LAW. Those who received the law on Sinai were in a transition stage. The Land of Promise was to be itself the blessing for which they looked. Now, the people having received possession of this, are taught that the blessing is still before them, and the curse also still impending over them. The obligations of the law are still vividly shown to be as incumbent on them as ever they were, and the annexed rewards and penalties are still beyond them "by the way where the sun goeth down." We are not set free from the law as a rule of conduct, and no reception of blessing in this world will save us from the curse if we become disobedient to the Divine precepts.

Among the curses pronounced by the Levites on Ebal, surrounded by six tribes, we may mark the first and last. The first is the curse against the man who made any graven image (Deut. xxvii. 15). Worship offered even to the true God in a carnal, unspiritual manner will not be accepted by Him. This same great truth was taught by Christ to the woman of Sychar ages after, as He sat wearied on the well at the foot of this hill, which He announced thus: "God is a Spirit, and they that worship Him must worship in spirit and in truth" (John iv. 24). The Romish use of images in worship is pronounced accursed here, as well as heathen idolatry.

Then, after the curses pronounced upon those who dishonour their parents, or who are guilty of acts of unkindness, oppression, impurity, or bloodshed, there follows a curse upon all who do not conform to and confirm the whole law (ver. 26). St. Paul quotes this penal enactment to prove that *all* men are guilty before God. These words honestly applied will have the effect of convincing even the most hardened of their sinfulness and exposure to just condemnation by the thrice-holy God. The moral law is a perfect whole, and he that offends in one point, St. James teaches, is guilty of all. He likens the law of liberty to a perfect, stainless mirror; and its beauty and value are alike marred, whether it be broken into two or into a hundred pieces.

To these curses the whole nation in its great assembly was required to express its assent by a loud "Amen." This was an entirely new departure in God's dealing with men. Jehovah now appealed to man's own moral sense of the justice of His law in its requirements and penalties. Man is called upon to justify his Maker in his sentence against sinners; God is now to be justified in his speaking, and be cleared in his judging. It would seem that this will be also one of the features of the judgment of the Great Day. However terrible the doom of the finally impenitent, there will be none who will argue that it is unjust: the great assemblage of men and angels will give their solemn assent to the verdict and sentence of the Righteous Judge. The Divine procedure is now often arraigned at the bar of human judgment; but one of the elements of awful grandeur in the Great Day will consist in the multitudinous "Amens" of the assenting universe, closing all possibility of an appeal being ever again raised at the bar of conscience and equity against the sentences of doom pronounced from the Great White Throne.

ON MOUNT EBAL AN ALTAR WAS TO BE ERECTED TO JEHOVAH. Why on Ebal, the mount of the curse, which still stands barren and thorn-clad with its northern aspect, while Gerizim, facing the sun, is clad with verdure kept green all through the summer by perennial brooks of water, in harmony with its character as the Mount of Blessing? The answer is, that it was most fitting that the altar bearing the sacrifice to remove the curse should be erected on the very spot where the curse was pronounced. If men could earn the blessing proclaimed on Mount Gerizim, they required no sacrifice and no altar; it was because they had incurred the awful curse of a broken law that they stood in need of these. The altar on the hill of the curse taught the Jews settled in Canaan the same lesson that had been taught to their fathers in the wilderness by the brazen serpent on the pole, viz., that the curse which was aimed against the sinner with such deadly sting is now itself dead through the death of Jesus. Looking for acceptance on the Mount of Blessing we find it, strange to say, on the dark hill that frowns opposite to it. Looking to Jesus as the Holy Lamb of God, we find this innocent Lamb not leaping upon Gerizim, but lying killed upon Mount Ebal. And drawing near to examine the victim on the altar, we see the Lamb ascending to the Throne of God, and in its place hangs a serpent on a pole—poisonous, fiery, deadly, but now itself a dead curse, a serpent of cold brass, and not of fiery fang any more—for on the cross "Christ hath redeemed us from the curse of the Law, being made a curse for us; for it is written, Cursed is every one that hangeth on a tree" (Gal. iii. 10–13). As we gaze upon Moses' pole with the uplifted serpent, and Calvary's cross with the " handwriting of ordinances that was against us " nailed to it, over the head of the crucified Lamb of God, "believing, we rejoice to see the curse remove."

This altar erected on Mount Ebal had also a connection with the loud "Amens" of the people. He who gave the Law did not require men to assent to its awful sentences, *except* IN FULL VIEW OF THE ATONING SACRIFICE —the provision made for the removal of the curse. Thus we see that the altar built upon Ebal, the hill of the curse, becomes one of the most instructive Gospel sermons in Scripture.

Moses further ordered that "great stones" should be erected on Mount Ebal, that these should be plastered over, and that on them should be inscribed "all the words of this law." The Ten Commandments were preserved as inscribed by Moses on the two stone tables ; but in addition to these, it would seem that possibly the whole ceremonial law of the Jewish nation, along with the appended curses and blessings, were to be recorded here. This inscription has long since perished, perhaps crumbled into dust through the lapse of time; but in any case, according to the determined purpose of God, whose own Son, having "forgiven us all trespasses, has *blotted out* the handwriting of ordinances that was against us, which was contrary to us, and took it out of the way, nailing it to his cross." The curse incurred by us, and pronounced against us, fell on Christ. Even on Him it did not rest, for He carried it away "into a land of forgetfulness." He is now once more most blessed for ever ; and we, too, inherit his blessing, being "not under the Law, but under Grace."

Another lesson taught on Mount Ebal by the requirement that the altar was to be built of unhewn stones (Deut. xxvii. 5), is, that IT WAS CONTRARY TO THE WILL OF GOD THAT HE SHOULD BE "WORSHIPPED BY ART OR MAN'S DEVICE." Though a brazen altar had already been in use, the people are here bidden revert to a simple altar of

undressed stones. There may here be a figurative reference
to Christ, who is our Altar, as well as Sacrifice and Priest,
being as "a stone cut without hands." But there is certainly
a pre-intimation of the simplicity of acceptable New Testament worship, and that everything of the nature of man's
device is to be eschewed in our worship of the Divine
Being.

Nearly 250 years after the impressive ceremony under
Joshua, when Gideon, the great Israelitish judge, had died,
and Abimelech, whose mother belonged to this town of
Shechem, having slain his seventy brethren, had been made
king here (Judges ix. 6–20), and doubtless thought that the
power of the magistracy, which was now in his own hand,
would shield him from the curse of the law he had violated,
Jotham, the youngest brother, having escaped, climbed
Gerizim ; and, with his clear, young voice, shouted to the
city of Shechem his parable of the trees choosing the thistle
for their king. Though the echoes of the Levites' curses
had long died away, and the frescoed writing on the plastered stones was faint, perhaps obliterated, we are told that
"God rendered the wickedness of Abimelech, and all the
evil of the men of Shechem upon their heads, and upon
them came the curse" (vers. 56, 57). The curse is sure to
fall upon law-breakers in the course of Providence, or at
the final judgment, even though they escape the sword of
the magistrate.

We cannot close our reflections on Ebal and Gerizim
without recalling again that wonderful conversation of Jesus
with the Samaritan woman at Jacob's well in their neighbourhood. He proved that the curse pronounced so long
ago was still operative when He said to her : "Go, call thy
husband, and come hither," and she felt its sharpness entering
her soul when she cried : "He told me all that ever I did."
But He also showed that the blessing was operative still, in
greater fulness than ever, when He spoke the memorable

words, " He that drinketh of the water that I shall give him shall never thirst ; but the water that I shall give him shall be in him a well of water springing up into everlasting life." This living water flows more abundantly from Christ's cross than do the many springs and streams under the shadow of Gerizim's blessings and Ebal's altar.

It is well that we should ask ourselves whether we have realized that a blessing and a curse are set before us as the inevitable award of our obedience or disobedience to the Divine law.   Have our consciences assented to the justice of the Divine condemnation of all whose conduct and heart are not fully conformable to the holy law ?   And have we learned that as transgressors of the law, we can only escape its penalty and curse by these being borne for us by Another, who has exhausted the curse for sinners, and transfers to them the blessing which was his by birthright, and by the merits of his life of holy obedience ?

X

𝔐ount 𝔊ilboa
The Mount of the Dark
Life-ending.

I Samuel xxxi. 8.

GILBOA is the name of a small detached mountain range situated between the eastern end of the plain of Jezreel and the Jordan valley. The city of Jezreel lay at the western end of the range, which rises to a moderate height. Shunem and Endor lay north of Gilboa across the valley of Jezreel towards little Hermon. While David's imprecation that neither dew nor rain should fall on this hill must be taken as a poetical figure flowing from the deep stirring of his spirit, Dean Stanley describes it as in harmony with the "bare, bleak, and jagged ridge, with its one green strip of table-land, where probably the last struggle was fought—the more bare and bleak from its unusual contrast with the fertile plain from which it springs."

Like Hor and Pisgah, Gilboa was the scene of the close of a distinguished man's life. As Aaron had inaugurated the priesthood, and Moses the prophetic office, so did Saul inaugurate the kingly rank in the Hebrew nation. But oh, how different his death from theirs! Gilboa was no mount either of goodly prospect or of happy retrospect. The retrospect of the life ended here was dark indeed ; and he would be bold who should assert that the prospect for the other world was bright.

There is a tragic fascination about the suicide of the king—

> O Saul,
> How ghastly didst thou look on thine own sword,
> Expiring on Gilboa !

the effect of which is enhanced by the furtive consultation with the witch Endor on the previous night. For whether we take this to be an imposition practised by the spiritualistic medium, or an impersonation of Samuel by some evil spirit (as Luther and Calvin held), or a real apparition of the wraith of the deceased judge, the weird glamour of the scene remains the same. The last supposition agrees best with the dignity and truth of the oracle, "To-morrow shalt thou and thy sons be with me."

The execution by David of the young Amalekite for interposing to hasten the prostrate monarch's death, according to his own confession, teaches us THE VALUE AND SACREDNESS OF LIFE, and that no man is justified in hurrying any of his fellows into the presence of his Maker, even with his own consent, or at his own request, to shorten dying agonies. There is a natural tendency to regard this as permissible. The Hindoo exposes his aged parent on the bosom of the river Ganges to shorten the days of which in his suffering he would sigh, "I have no pleasure in them." The watcher by the dying couch of a loved one may be tempted to ask for the administration of some drug that would still that fluttering breast, and close in the peace of death those fevered eyeballs that roll so restlessly. It may not be. These latest weary hours are allotted by Him who gave the life; it may be to communicate the pardon, the sanctifying grace, and the teaching needed to fit the departing spirit to meet its God.

We are taught also that IN THE PRESENCE OF DEATH ALL PRIVATE WRONGS MUST BE FORGOTTEN, all jealousies must perish. David had in the most magnanimous spirit refrained from avenging himself on the man who hunted for his life, scorning the counsel of those who urged him to slay him when he was in his power, by saying, "His day shall come to die, or he shall descend into battle and perish." This day had now come, and we find David mourning over

Saul's death in one of the most beautiful elegies ever penned. We talk of the defects of the religion of the Old Testament saints, but when we observe the way in which many professing Christians speak after their death of those who have wronged them, must we not own that in some points of morals they are far outstripped by this Jewish saint?

In this ode David celebrates all that was good in Saul's character and glorious in his reign, allowing to drop out of view what was ungodly, cruel, and vindictive. Saul's bravery, his handsome bearing, his services to his country, his love for his son Jonathan—are woven into the sonnet; and all that was passionate, dark, and diabolic, is allowed to sink out of sight. This elegy has no religious element in it, not even pointing the moral which Saul's dark death naturally suggested; and its inclusion in the sacred writings, as well as the universal approval of it by the moral judgment of men, shows that the gifts of music and song were not intended to be confined to religious subjects, as some earnest Christians mistakenly hold. At the same time its redolence of forgiveness and magnanimity teaches us that our ordinary speaking and acting should be fragrant with a Christ-like spirit.

Mount Gilboa witnesses that ONE EVENT HAPPENS TO THE RIGHTEOUS AND TO THE WICKED. Saul and Jonathan fell together in the same battle. It is the life and not the death that puts a difference between the just and the unjust. These two warriors, father and son, died together—the one an embodiment of all that is true, lovely, and generous; the other an embodiment of all that is false, selfish, and cruel. By the same blood-stained path they entered together the unseen world, where Samuel was; but we can hardly dare to conclude, however closely united in their lives and undivided in their deaths, that no separation was interposed between them in the world of spirits. But the marked reticence as to this, both in Samuel's solemn oracle and David's touching elegy, forbids us to speak rashly concerning the eternal state of any individual, and bids us leave this reverently to the righteous decision of the Judge of all the earth, who judges according to every man's work, and who may even in his dying moments grant pardon, and acceptance, and a new heart to the vilest of sinners, without granting the opportunity to the dying man of giving a dying testimony.

Mount Gilboa bears beautiful witness to THE STRENGTH OF DISINTERESTED LOVE. The mutual love of David and Jonathan redeems the roughness of the times in which they lived ; indeed, it would adorn that long-looked-for age of gold,

> When the new heavens and ransomed earth,
>   Seen by prophetic dreamer,
> Emerging from their second birth,
>   Greet their returned Redeemer.

Jonathan, the heir of the crown, being removed by death, the way is left clear for David to ascend the throne, to which he had long ago been designated and anointed by the heaven-commissioned prophet. Yet there is not, in the outpouring of that royal heart, even the most subdued tone of satisfaction that so it is. There is here a silent but very emphatic rebuke to the spirit which we sometimes see evinced by persons who, when death has removed those to whose wealth, and it may be titles, they succeed, can hardly, under the solemn garb and approved expressions of mourning, conceal their gratification at the acquisition of means or position which the decease has brought to them. Here again, does not the old economy administer a stinging rebuke to the spirit so prevalent in modern civilization, and even in modern Christianity ?

If Mount Gilboa, according to David's dirge, was to bear "no fields of offerings," but to lie under a blight of barrenness, it has in a higher sense borne some of the noblest offerings ever presented to God or man ; for not only did King Saul and his sons here freely sacrifice their lives at the shrine of duty and at the call of their country, but here it was that David presented an offering of unselfish admiration for a dead foe who had bitterly persecuted him, and of self-forgetful affection and grief for a dead friend, such as has evoked the wondering applause of countless generations.

But Gilboa admonishes us that SOME LIVES WHICH BEGIN WITH GREAT PROMISE, LIKE SAUL'S, ENTIRELY FAIL TO BRING FORTH THE FRUIT THAT MIGHT HAVE BEEN LOOKED FOR. In Saul's youth we discern in his character the grace of humility. It is recorded that "he hid himself among the stuff" when called forth to be proclaimed king. This beautiful virtue soon withered away, and in its place we find self-assertion, pride, and rancorous hatred of such as he imagined threatened his supremacy. Then, too, he associated himself with the Lord's people, for when he returned home from his election to the throne, "there went with him a band of men whose hearts God had touched" ; while on the night preceding his death we find him seeking the company of one who practised those black arts which Israel's holy God had distinctly condemned. At his coronation he exercised great self-restraint, and forbearance towards those who opposed his elevation to the throne. So entirely did this virtue disappear, that no character in history is more disfigured by violent outbreaks of uncontrolled passion, and by cruel plotting against the innocent youth whom he mistakenly regarded as a menace to his authority. All this early promise was nipped in the bud, and his whole moral character steadily deteriorated as time wore on. Saul was also naturally open to the impressions of religion, and was far from regardless of its claims ; but his suicide on Gilboa was a tragic end to a life that had been all along more or less influenced by religious impulses, but not by sustained piety or true moral principles.

Saul's religious experiences are of such a character as, in view of their empty results, carefully to lead us to inquire whether our impressions regarding spiritual things are deeper and more enduring than were his. We are told that after he parted from Samuel, when he had poured the holy oil upon him, "God gave him another heart"; but the sequel shows that it was not "a new heart." On various occasions he came under the influence of the Spirit of God. More than once he prophesied among those who were similarly moved—at one of these times laying aside his royal apparel (1 Sam. xix. 24) and falling apparently into a state of religious trance. These manifestations led the people to say, "Is Saul also among the prophets?"

Just before his death he said to the shade of Samuel, which the female clairvoyant had called up, that "God answered him no more, neither by prophets nor by dreams" (ch. xxviii. 15). This implies that Saul had not been without answers to prayer during his earlier life, and that now he was conscious of a woful difference in this respect.

Like Herod the Tetrarch in later times, he entertained a regard for the prophets of the Lord, whose messages appealed to his conscience, but whose counsels he did not fully carry out. Gilboa is a monument from whose summit we will do well to take a retrospect of a life which was very fruitless in what constitutes man's chief end, and marks the dark close of the moral struggle of a nature which yielded to its lower impulses. His goodness, alas! was as "a morning cloud, and as the early dew that goeth away." His religion degenerated at last into sheer superstition and spiritualism, leaving his nature as dry and barren of all good as the dewless rocks of Gilboa.

The history, which opened with an attractive interview

with Samuel, after many shifting scenes of dramatic impressiveness, closes with another interview with the departed spirit of the same great prophet, full of weird and fascinating interest, the culmination of which is the king's confession, that now God had forsaken him. At the outset of his public career Samuel had said to him, "God is with thee"; at its close Saul said to him who had been his faithful spiritual instructor, but whose admonitions he had neglected, "God is departed from me." Dying, he leaves us with the impression of his having received the grace of God in vain.

Before you turn from Mount Gilboa and its lessons, let me ask you, my reader, Is your religion prompted by pure motives, and regulated by godly principle? Is it used by you as a cloak for covetousness, or self-aggrandisement, or any other worldly end? Is your piety deepening as time goes on? Or is it degenerating, losing its influence over your conduct, and threatening to evaporate altogether, like morning dew?

Are you harbouring in your heart any lurking seeds of jealousy, and cherishing hatred such as made Saul's life so unhappy and so injurious to himself and others? Or do you allow any evil temper to rise up unchecked?

Do you value and cherish the privilege of friendship? Do you know anything of such self-sacrificing love as subsisted between Jonathan and David? And do you enjoy the more than brotherly love of that Friend, who, though He was the Heir of all, yet laid down his life that we, who had been his enemies, might share his inheritance, and be advanced to his throne?

XI

Mount Carmel

The Mountain of the Vindication.

1 KINGS xviii. 19–21.

CARMEL is the name of a mountainous range in Central Palestine, within the ancient tribe of Asher, which runs east and west for some fifteen miles, terminating in a striking promontory 600 feet high, which juts into the Mediterranean Sea. The range, though nowhere lofty, rises to nearly thrice this altitude ; and the scene of Elijah's conflict with the priests of Baal is traditionally located on a natural rock-terrace towards its eastern extremity, which bears the name of El-muhrakah, The Sacrifice. Here stands an ancient square building of massive hewn stones, reared upon the supposed site of Elijah's altar.

Carmel signifies a Park, or fruitful field, and this name was evidently assigned to it from the richness of its pasture, the abundance and variety of its flowers, and the beauty of its trees. The range separates two of the fairest and most fertile plains of Palestine, sloping down gradually towards Sharon on the south, and descending more abruptly to the plain of Esdraelon on the north, through which winds the tortuous channel of the river Kishon, approaching the base of the cliffs near the traditional site of Elijah's altar. Here, also, springs a perennial fountain, from which it is supposed the barrels were filled, which by the prophet's orders were thrice emptied on the wood laid on the altar, until the trench surrounding it was filled with water. All the heights of Carmel are clothed with wood in an open park-like

manner, the evergreen oak being the commonest tree ;
while long, deep ravines, travellers tell us, of singular
wildness, wind down the mountain-sides filled with tangled
copse, fragrant with hawthorn, myrtle, and jasmine, and
resonant with the murmur of tiny brooks and the songs of
birds.   The open glades are carpeted with green grass, and
spangled with myriads of wild flowers of every hue.   It is
no wonder, therefore, that the name of Carmel became a
synonym for luxuriance of vegetation and picturesque
beauty.

It is not, however, its remarkable natural beauty which
has endeared Mount Carmel to the Church of Christ, but
the fact that on this range of hills was made an ever-
memorable vindication of the claim of Jehovah to be
the Ruler of Nature and the Hearer of Prayer.   We are apt
heedlessly to take it for granted that our religion has been
associated during its whole history with a constant succes-
sion of miracles, that these were its constant evidences ; and
a misgiving sometimes arises when the Christian apologist
has to confess that he cannot appeal to new miracles in
support of his faith.   Such a view is quite mistaken.   The
appeal usually made by psalmists and prophets, on behalf
of the claims of Jehovah to be the Supreme God, is to the
uniformity of the laws of nature as testifying to his eternal
power and God-head, and not to miraculous interferences
with those laws.

Miracles are confined almost entirely to four well-
marked epochs, when it was necessary that the Author of
revelation should afford irrefutable evidence that He was the
Creator and Providential Ruler of the world.   The first of
those periods occurred when Jehovah formed a Church on
earth, and entrusted it with a revelation of his will, under
Moses, and his successor Joshua.   Miracles were next
vouchsafed, as the credentials of the true religion, at the
crisis when the impressive scene on Carmel finds its place ;

when the worshippers of Jehovah were engaged in life-and-death struggle with the votaries of Baal-worship.

This form of heathenism, or Nature-worship, seems once to have overspread well-nigh the whole world, leaving its impress on the names of many localities in our own islands. It also most prejudicially influenced the Christian worship of the early centuries, and has depraved the ritual and doctrine of the Romish Church, which seems to have received the name of Babylon in the Apocalypse from the fact that this false faith originated in that great city and kingdom. Elijah was the courageous upholder and restorer of the true faith ; and he and his successor, Elisha, were gifted with the power of working miracles as credentials of their Divine mission. We do not again find miracles occurring (except sporadically) until the ministry of Jesus Christ. If Judaism was certified in this way, it was important that Christianity should possess a similar attestation. After Christ's ascension, we find the apostles accredited in the same manner to complete the revelation of God to men, by working miracles as great as, or greater than, any that had taken place in the previous dispensations. Unless a crisis in the history of the Christian Church should recur like the second of those enumerated, there seems no reason to expect a renewal of miraculous intervention.

By the events that transpired under Elijah on Mount Carmel we are taught that THE PEOPLE OF GOD MUST RENDER TO HIM AN UNDIVIDED WORSHIP. Those who advocated the worship of Nature, or of Baal—who may be regarded as a personification of the powers or laws of nature—both in their early and later efforts to extend this false religion, appear to have been anxious to engraft it upon the true faith, thus forming a compromise between the two. The mass of the nation of Israel had conformed to the new rites (which had been introduced from Phœnicia by Queen Jezebel, and had the patronage of the court and of the easily-swayed King

Ahab), but were not prepared entirely to renounce the God of their fathers. To them the uncompromising prophet addressed the solemn appeal, " How long halt ye between two opinions ? If Jehovah be God, follow Him ! But if Baal, then follow him ! "

Elijah, addressing the crowds of his countrymen assembled upon the slopes of Carmel, declared to them that this religion of compromise would not do, and that they must choose between Baal and Jehovah. They could not remain un-decided on such a momentous question. It would not do to assume the attitude of opportunists, waiting to see how the current of national sentiment would ultimately flow. Such a course, so congenial to human nature, is unworthy of those who are endowed with faculties of intellect and judgment. Elijah set himself, as Joshua had done in an earlier age, to bring his hearers to the point of decision, exclaiming, "Choose ye this day whom ye will serve ! " The halting attitude is the most unsatisfactory of all posi-tions and the most perilous. It imposes on those who do not understand it, and ruins those who do. It deceives the halting one himself, and affects with loathing Him who calls Himself a Jealous GOD.

There is nothing to which men are naturally more averse than to be brought to the point of decision ; and the success of all great prophets, reformers, and revival preachers, has lain in their ability to lead men to it. In Baal-worship, whether practised in Babylon, or in Palestine, or in our own sea-girt islands at Stonehenge or Stennis, there was no inculcation of the moral law with its pure precepts and severe penalties ; no provision made for a holy walk in fellowship with a personal God ; no proclamation of forgive-ness ; no manifestation of the Divine Love ; no promise of an answer to the suppliant's prayer. Yet the multitude wavered then, as multitudes halt and waver still, between the two religions, trying to serve two masters. Conscience, memory, judgment, principle, and the written Word, all pleaded on the side of Elijah; while fashion, fear, worldly compliance, and regard to temporal interests, strenuously pressed their pleas against him.

Mount Carmel gives testimony to the great Protestant principle of THE RIGHT AND DUTY OF FREE ENQUIRY AND PRIVATE JUDGMENT in the great subject of religion. This vast assembly came as spectators, and did not expect to be addressed directly by the far-famed preacher. They regarded the religion of the land as a matter to be settled by the rulers of the nation, or perhaps as a controversy falling to be decided by the rival sets of prophets. They were interested in watching how the claims of these competing systems would be adjudicated on. But Elijah carried the appeal from both these judicatories, the ecclesiastical and the secular, directly to the conscience and judgment of individuals, calling upon them to pronounce their verdict in answer to the impassioned yet reasonable appeal, "How long halt ye between two opinions?" Do we not require at present to listen to the public testimony given on Carmel to the principle, that on the individual rests the ultimate responsibility of forming and avowing his own decision in regard to religion, and that he cannot divest himself of this responsibility by devolving it on either civil or ecclesiastical rulers? These have important duties in regard to religion, but they must not come between the soul and its God.

Another lesson taught on Mount Carmel is that THE GOD OF THE BIBLE IS THE ALMIGHTY CREATOR. Creation and Providence are the operations of Jehovah, who speaks to us in the revelation of Grace. While the regularity of the laws of nature proclaims the character and natural attributes of the Most High, his intervention in controlling these laws at a special juncture proves Him to be a personal God who holds intercourse with his intelligent and morally

responsible creatures.   Denial of the occurrence of miracles
is nearly tantamount to the denial of a personal Deity ; and
the present tendency to dispute the evidence of miracles
is, so far, a rejecting of credentials which it was reasonable
to expect his messengers to produce.   Moral and spiritual
credentials as seals of apostleship are certainly higher than
any that are merely physical, but the absence of the latter
would seriously weaken the force of the former.   All God's
true servants, like Elijah, claim that the material universe
is as much the work of God as the spiritual.   Elijah's
challenge to the prophets of Baal to call down fire from
heaven was peculiarly appropriate, for the elements of fire
and light were specially associated with this form of Nature-
worship.   Any dissociating of the two spheres of the manifestation of the Divine power and presence is inimical to
spiritual religion.

The believer regards the laws of nature simply as the
ordinary means by which the Creator carries out his will in
the material universe.   Miracles are the extraordinary
methods by which on special occasions He carries out the
same will.   The opponents of miracles most unreasonably
deny to the Supreme Being the power and liberty of modifying, suspending, and counteracting in every portion of his
universe, by the direct exertion of his will, or by the employ-
ment of higher agencies, those natural laws which the
objector himself is daily modifying or counteracting in his
own surroundings, when by the spontaneity of his free will,
or by the use of some other natural force, such as steam
or electricity, he controls or interrupts the action of gravitation, or any other natural law.   But miracles are not confined to supernatural interventions by the Supreme Will.
On the contrary, many of the miracles recorded in Scripture,
like both of those wrought on Mount Carmel, consist simply
in occurrences produced by the ordinary laws of nature
at specially designated times in answer to prayer, or in

fulfilment of a Divine prediction. Fire and rain are constantly descending from the sky ; and the miraculous element here consisted in their descent being timed to coincide exactly with the hour of Elijah's supplication.

The Apostle James points us to another lesson taught on Carmel, viz., that " THE EFFECTUAL FERVENT PRAYER OF A RIGHTEOUS MAN AVAILETH MUCH." Jehovah was here vindicated as a personal, sentient, prayer-hearing God, interested in the condition of his worshippers, and ready to succour them when in distress. One of the main proofs of the existence, as well as the kindness, of Jehovah is that his ear is ever open to the cry of suppliants, and that He is ready to answer their petitions, when presented for things agreeable to his holy will. We are told that all flesh shall come to Him because He is the Hearer of prayer. It is told of the distinguished judge, Lord Jeffrey, that a Christian friend, concerned about his irreligious and sceptical sentiments, regularly sent him anonymously through the post the pointed tracts of the Monthly Tract Society, which his lordship as regularly threw into his waste-paper receptacle unread. But, on one occasion, having glanced at one in which the reader was urged not to continue in doubt as to the being of God without putting it to the test of earnest prayer, a test demanded throughout Scripture, Lord Jeffrey felt satisfied of the reasonableness of this line of proof. Resolving to apply this prayer-test to this greatest of all subjects, he also searched out and carefully pondered the tracts he had previously discarded, with the result that a marked and blessed change was wrought in him.

On Carmel we learn that TRUE AND SUCCESSFUL PRAYER MUST BE PROMPTED BY A DEEP SENSE OF NEED. Elijah went to the top of Mount Carmel, where Palestine's richest plains stretched in all their barrenness before his vision. He prayed with a sense of entire dependence upon God ; but before beginning to pray for rain, he first prayed for fire from heaven as a token that his sacrifice was accepted. All answers to prayer are granted for the sake of Christ, who offered Himself as "a sacrifice and an offering to God of a sweet-smelling savour"; and no time is lost by the suppliant in first asking that he and his prayer together may be accepted in Christ Jesus. Elijah on Carmel gave us a model of the order in which we ought to present our petitions. Let us ask first for some token and some bright assurance that God has accepted of Christ's sacrifice for us.

We should seek that the evidence of this given in the New Testament may be so applied to us, that we may enjoy full assurance of it. It is written, "He who spared not his own Son, but delivered Him up for us all, how shall He not *with Him* also freely give us all things?" The descent of the heavenly fire would strengthen Elijah's faith to plead for the descent of heaven's rain. The Holy Spirit came down once in the form of fire on the Day of Pentecost, and ever since He has been descending from the same opened heaven on his praying people, "as rain on the mown grass, and as showers that water the earth." It was an easier task for the prophet's faith to expect fire than rain from that burning sky overhead, and the flaming gifts of Pentecost, wonderful as they are, are perhaps more easily believed in than the abundant and continuous bestowal of life-giving rain of which we stand in such sore need.

Elijah, believing now that the longed-for rain would be vouchsafed, did not consider that all that he had to do was to wait till it arrived; but intimating to the monarch that it was coming, he ascended to the top of the hill, and casting himself on the ground, put his face between his knees. He assumed this posture not only in deep humility, but to prevent his fainting faith from being weakened by the sight of the blazing firmament overhead, or the burnt-up plains around him. It is safest for us to look away from everything to that God who alone can send the needed help.

We can almost hear him soliloquising, "My soul, wait thou only upon God, for my expectation is from Him." The Lord had given him a definite promise: "I will send rain upon the earth" (1 Kings xviii. 1); yet this did not make him remiss in praying, but gave him the more hopefulness and importunity in his entreaty. Seven distinct times he engaged in earnest supplication. Each time his hope deferred still sustained him against despair, until the servant returned from his seventh mission to the hilltop, not again with the heart-sickening message, "There is nothing," but with the gladdening words, "There ariseth a little cloud out of the sea, like a man's hand." Then the man of God knew that he had won his suit, and that his God, so rich in goodness, when He gave would give to him and his people as much as they needed. So, knowing well the bountiful nature of his God, he sent to Ahab the message: "Prepare thy chariot, and get thee down, that the rain stop thee not!" "In the meanwhile the heaven was black with clouds, and there was a great rain." Jehovah was gloriously vindicated in his being, his power, and his goodness.

It is well that we should remember, as the apostle James reminds us, that this man who so prevailed in prayer was not a perfectly sinless saint, but was, as his history shows, "a man subject to like passions as we are." But, while all men are commanded to pray and not to faint, while sinners are called upon at once to become suppliants, those who take upon themselves the holy office of intercessors for others, while by no means perfect, but marked by imperfections which may be patent to others as well as to themselves, must yet be "righteous men," in harmony with the Holy Being whose favour they are entreating, as well as in sympathy with men for whom they are interceding. The position of an intercessor is a peculiarly honourable and arduous one; and for one to fill effectively the office of a mediator, sanctified by the wonderful intercedings of such

chosen saints of God as Abraham, when he pleaded for
Sodom ; Moses, when he pleaded for the Israelites ; and
Paul, for his brethren according to the flesh—he must bear
something of the character of the Great Mediator Himself,
that Righteous One, whose wondrous intercessions for his
people are all-prevailing.

As we descend from Mount Carmel, let me ask you, my
reader, to consider that a solemn responsibility rests on
you to come to a personal decision on the great subject of
religion.

Are you rendering to God an undivided worship ? Or are
you endeavouring to effect a compromise between the
service of God and the service and love of the world, or
of mammon, or of self ?   Are you halting between two
opinions ? If so, how long do you intend continuing in this
attitude ?   Is it honouring to God, or safe for yourself ?

Do you believe that God is, and is a rewarder of them
that diligently seek Him ?   Have you learned to pray
for yourself earnestly, importunately, and expecting an
answer ? If so, do you try to pray also for others—to be
an intercessor ?

XII

Mount Lebanon

"That Goodly Mountain and Lebanon."

DEUT. iii. 25.

MOUNT LEBANON is the name of a great mountain mass on the extreme north of Palestine, consisting of two parallel ranges, about ninety miles in length, running nearly north and south. They enclose between them a fertile plain called the Bekâ, or Cœle-Syria. Of these, the western range alone bears in classical authors the name Lebanon ; that to the east being named Anti-Lebanon. This distinction is not made in the sacred writings, in which, however, the highest and southern summit of the eastern range is called Mount Hermon, and treated as a distinct mountain. It is not improbable that Moses' epithet, "that goodly mountain," applies to Hermon rather than to Lebanon proper ; but the characteristics of the two mountains are the same.

Lebanon rises from the Levant, whose waves lave its base, to an altitude of 10,000 feet, towering to just within the limits of perpetual snow, which caps its summit and extends some little way down in the gullies and crevasses on its north side. Its name, " White Mountain," seems, like the Alpine Mont Blanc, to be derived from its snowy peak, rather than from the whitish tint of its limestone rocks, which it shares with much of the scenery in Palestine.

This mountain far excels all those which have engaged our attention in its combination of majesty and beauty, whose union constitutes its distinctive "goodliness." Horeb, Sinai, and Hor, like huge mountain skeletons, with no rounded flesh-like covering, and unvestured by vegetation, impress the beholder with a sense of savage grandeur, desolation, and death. Carmel possesses beauty and fertility, but lacks majesty ; but here we gaze on a mountain as sublime as beautiful—

> Whose head in wintry grandeur towers,
> And whitens with eternal sleet,
> While summer, in a vale of flowers,
> Is sleeping rosy at his feet.

Lebanon differs from other Scripture hills in this : that no striking event of religious significance took place on its slopes or summit. Yet it is constantly referred to by prophets and psalmists, and they agree in drawing from it important religious instruction.

Lebanon was THE GREAT BARRIER WHICH BOUNDED THE LAND OF ISRAEL'S INHERITANCE to the north. The lot of his people had been chosen for them by their Lord who cared for and loved them ; yet, as Israel when chosen by Jehovah was "the fewest of all peoples," so their land was among the least of all lands. It was not a land that could be extended in any direction, its extreme limits being strictly defined by the blue Mediterranean on the west, by yellow or red deserts on the south and east, and by the great mass of Lebanon on the north. We are taught here a lesson of contentment with our own condition, with our home and its surroundings, with the measure of means and influence assigned to us by God. There is room for the exercise of honourable ambition and enterprise by all ; but these must be guided into the directions indicated by Providence, and neither as individuals nor as nations may we covet possessions of any kind belonging to our neighbours. The spirit of discontent with what the good God has given us richly to enjoy, and grasping at what He has bestowed upon others, is a source of great disquiet and danger, alike to the individual, the family, and the nation.

We all have our Lebanons hemming us in, and are warned against trying to remove such landmarks, or to trespass on that from which they shut us out.

But while Lebanon formed a boundary which Israel was never to cross, along with the other natural limits of Palestine it constituted A GREAT PHYSICAL BULWARK, protecting the land from invasion.

Except for the sea, the deserts, and the mountain which on all sides hemmed them in, the Israelites would never have been able to hold their country against the powerful empires by which they were surrounded ; and it was at last captured only because through their sins they had provoked their God to forsake them. One has only to look, as the writer has done, at the narrow road cut in the rock at the sea-washed base of Lebanon, beside the Lycus or Dog-river, with its inscriptions of successive conquering armies, to see how easily men, nerved by the fear of God and animated by his presence, could have turned back the marshalled hosts which once and again invaded their land by that fateful path. So shall we also find that the very restrictions that limit our advancement in life may prove our best defence. Such limitations are fortifications.

In Lebanon we are confronted by Nature in one of her great masterpieces, and are reminded by the Hebrew prophets that Nature also is the handiwork of the God of revelation, that the Creator is also the Redeemer, and that natural law, as well as moral and spiritual law, is the expression of his will. It can hardly be said that natural law rules in the spiritual world, but it can be maintained that the analogy between the laws of these diverse worlds is so close as to convince any reverent observer that they are inspired by one Mind. The beautiful Parables of our Saviour attest this ; and Mount Lebanon was selected by the Jewish prophets as furnishing instructive examples of THE ANALOGY BETWEEN NATURE AND GRACE. As it was a boundary between the people of God and the surrounding nations, who yet met on its lofty ridges, and in its sheltered valleys, engaged in the common labour of furnishing and framing from its renowned cedars materials for the Temple which Solomon was building in Jerusalem to the true God, so standing at the boundary between Nature and Grace it has become their meeting-place. Here we see that there is no antagonism between these realms, but that they are in true harmony.

On the ground of this analogy the prophets point to the majesty, strength, and firm roots of Lebanon's cedars as indications and pledges that grace in the heart of man should possess the same characteristics. Of Him who was the fairest of the sons of men, the Church sang in her Old Testament Canticle, "His countenance is like Lebanon, excellent as the cedars." The Lord through his servant Hosea declares that his Church when revived by the dews of his grace should " cast forth her roots as Lebanon." We are pointed to these " cedars of Lebanon which the Lord hath planted " as a picture of THE DEEP-ROOTED AND ENDURING NATURE OF GRACE in the renewed heart. It is no ephemeral growth with merely a surface-hold of man's nature, but is so deeply rooted as to be independent alike of summer droughts and winter blasts. Oh, that grace may have such a firm possession of our heart, that this image may be a real portrait and not a caricature !

In Hosea's prophecy Ephraim is represented as seizing upon the image of the cedar, in his interjection, " I am like a green fir-tree : " if there is in me something of evergreen foliage, there is, alas ! nothing of fruitfulness. To this the Lord replied, " From Me is thy fruit found." The "glory of Lebanon " consisted as much in THE VARIETY AND RICH-NESS OF ITS FRUIT-BEARING TREES, as in the majesty and eternity of its cedars ; and the Great Husbandman looks that his people should produce the fruits of the Spirit in varied profusion. The olives and mulberries, citrons, vines and apples, and all fruits of garden and orchard on Lebanon, are fit yet faint images of the "love, joy, peace, long-suffering, gentleness, goodness, faith, meekness, temperance," which are produced in the garden of man's heart, under the dews of the Holy Spirit and the shining of the Sun of Righteousness.

But in the Lebanon the fruit-bearing is THE RESULT OF CAREFUL AND LONG-CONTINUED CULTURE. The building of the terraces in which the fruit-trees are planted has been, we are told, a work of immense labour, and all the toilsome and patience-taxing processes of agriculture are selected by the sacred writers as figures of the prolonged providential and gracious processes by which the hard and stony heart is transformed into a garden of the Lord, fruitful in every good work. Nature shared in the fall of her lord, the curse of sterility being, for his transgression, pronounced over her; and it may, therefore, be expected that the methods of reclaiming physical nature and human nature will have a close resemblance. We are not to expect these rich fruits of grace to be produced spontaneously, or even suddenly, in barren hearts and lives, but are to exercise the "long patience" of the husbandman in waiting for their production, whether in others or in ourselves. The sweet singer of Israel compares God's people in the world to a handful of corn on the top of the mountains, the fruit whereof should shake like Lebanon, and whose citizens should flourish like the grass. The Church, which, if fruitful at all, the world regards but as a poor patch of mountain-sown corn, should bear such heavy crops, that the breeze, rustling the ears, should sound like the blast tossing the mighty boughs of Lebanon's cedars. But for reproductiveness and permanence, David likens the Church to the grass that clothes this mountain's vales and slopes.

John Ruskin testifies to the aptness of this illustration

when he writes : "You roll the grass, and it is stronger next day; you mow it, and it multiplies its shoots as if it were grateful; you tread upon it, and it only sends up richer perfume. Spring comes, and it rejoices with all the earth, waving its soft depth of fruitful strength; winter comes, and it will not pine and mourn, and turn colourless and leafless. It is always green, and is only the brighter and gayer for the hoar-frost." May Christ's Church exhibit these qualities in the present, as she has been enabled to do in the past !

Under the figure of the scent of Lebanon, the PERVASIVE SWEETNESS OF TRUE PIETY is set forth. "His beauty shall be as the olive-tree, and his smell as Lebanon." We are admonished that our graces be *attractive* as well as productive. A native of Lebanon noted how the prophet drew his image from "the abundance of aromatic things and odoriferous flowers" in his mountain home, the perfume of which meets the traveller as he enters these valleys. Or, as another resident in Palestine writes :

> Sweet are the flowers which grow around
> The paths where Jesus trod ;
> The fragrance of those holy fields
> Blest by the feet of God. [1]

And if their scent is fugitive, we are reminded that the power of grace to communicate a heavenly fragrance to the surrounding social atmosphere is to be permanent, in the words, "the scent thereof shall be as the wine of Lebanon." Many Christians forget or ignore the attractive power and flower-like fragrance of piety, and are not careful to exhibit this in their daily conduct, which is very detrimental to their influence for good.

One more element in the "goodliness" of Lebanon was THE ABUNDANCE OF STREAMS that rose on its heights,

---

[1] If Jesus is not recorded to have visited Lebanon proper, He on a memorable occasion climbed Hermon, which is the loftiest summit of the whole range.

watered its valleys, and sent rivers of life to the surrounding lands—the Jordan flowing south through Palestine, the Barrada (Abana and Pharpar) flowing east to Damascus, the Kadisha and the classical Adonis flowing to the north and west. The "streams from Lebanon," therefore, celebrated in Holy Writ (Cant. iv. 15), were used as an instructive metaphor of the manner in which the Church of God should send forth streams of influence and life into regions that had been as valleys of death. The stream from the Smitten Rock shows us that such supplies of life must flow from Jesus Christ; but the "streams from Lebanon" teach us that from his Church also such living waters flow forth. Jesus Himself is the Source of the water of life; but when we have come to Him and drawn out of his fulness, the water which He gives us is to be "in us a well of water springing up into everlasting life," so that out of us, too, "there shall flow rivers of living water."

While, then, it is our privilege to pray, "to speak to the Rock to give forth his water," it is our duty to send streams of grace and beneficence in all directions round about us, near and far. As Lebanon, drinking freely of falling snows and rains, and distilling dews, freely disperses streams to populous lands and cities, so let us, having received freely, learn to give freely.

As we now descend from Lebanon, let me ask, Have you learned, in whatsoever state you are, therewith to be content, and not to murmur at the limits by which Providence bounds your lot?

Do you discern God's hand in nature around you, alike in the great and small?

Are your graces deep-rooted in your nature, and productive of good fruits in your life?

Do you commend your religion by making it attractive? And are you seeking freely to dispense to others the life which you have received?

XIII.

Mount Zion

The Hill of the Home Sanctuary.

I CHRON. xi. 5-7.

MOUNT ZION has a peculiar interest in the eyes of Christians, for its name has been transferred from the Old Testament vocabulary to that of the New Testament, and has become a synonym for the Church of Christ. Our hymns are often called Songs of Zion. Round this hill there cling many sacred associations that have always been prized by the Christian Church, and from its history we may learn many lessons which it is important that we should not let slip.

Mount Zion was the last and strongest fortress of the old pagan inhabitants of Palestine, yet it became the very centre and seat of the Lord's Kingdom in the earth. This almost impregnable stronghold was held until the days of King David by those who knew not the true God. So strong was it that they boasted that it could be held by a garrison of the blind and lame against all the flower of Israel's chivalry. It was captured by Joab, who himself, alas! gave no evidence of being a subject of Divine grace, though belonging outwardly to the people of God.

An all-wise Providence sometimes uses persons who are not, apparently, true subjects of the King of kings, as instruments for overthrowing ancient and powerful systems of error, cruelty, or vice. These have frequently been overturned by warriors and statesmen who did not profess to be true Christians. These " men of the world, which have their portion in this life," were, in the words of the psalmist, " the hand of God." When Jehovah decided to break the power of Babylon which itself had been "the hammer of the whole earth," He raised against it "the spirit of the kings of the Medes," of whom He said, "Thou art my battle-axe and weapons of war, for with thee will I break in pieces the nations, and with thee will I destroy kingdoms."

While Zion was captured by Joab, it became the residence of David, the "man after God's own heart." In his palace on this hill, Israel's monarch of song wrote many of those psalms which soon displaced the heathen odes and vicious songs of Palestine, and which have since supplanted strains of devil-worship and debauchery throughout large regions of the world; so that we are constrained to exclaim, "O the depth of the riches both of the wisdom and knowledge of God; how unsearchable are his judgments, and his ways past finding out!" Let none then of God's children give way to despondency, far less sink into despair, because some evil holds out against their individual efforts, or even resists the united assaults of Christ's Church. Satan's stronghold which frowns defiance at you, and seems to scorn, even to ridicule your efforts to achieve its overthrow, will assuredly yield ere long, and may yet become a centre whence you and others, perhaps through many generations, will go forth to win fresh victories for your all-conquering King.

The hymns of David have struck the keynote for many of our modern sacred singers in celebrating the privileges of Zion.

> Glorious things of thee are spoken,
>   Zion, city of our God;
> He whose word cannot be broken
>   Formed thee for his own abode.
>
> Blest inhabitants of Zion,
>   Washed in the Redeemer's blood—
> Jesus, whom their souls rely on,
>   Makes them kings and priests to God.
>   NEWTON.

Mount Zion witnesses to THE BLESSINGS ATTENDANT
UPON HOME RELIGION; to the desirableness of having a
church in the house.   King David was deterred from bringing the Ark of the Covenant home to himself when it
was fetched from Kirjath-jearim, because when the oxen
stumbled as they carried it on the new cart, Uzza, one of
the two brothers who were driving, put forth his hand to
hold the Ark, and was smitten by God for his error.
David was afraid to have the Ark of such a holy God, so
jealous of his honour, brought into his house, and he
carried it to the house of Obed-edom, the Gittite.   Only
after it was observed that during the three months of its
sojourn there "God blessed the house of Obed-edom and
all that he had, because of the Ark of God," was the king
induced to prepare an abode for it in his palace.

A marked place was assigned to home religion by Moses,
as well as by the patriarchs; but perhaps the most impressive picture of it is the establishment of the shrine of
Israel's worship in the royal home, in the days of King
David.   It teaches us that Divine worship in the family is
not less august, acceptable, or effective, than in the sanctuary,
and that when it is duly observed, it brings a blessing
upon the household.   At the same time the sad history of
some of David's sons reminds us that the possession of the
means of grace does not of itself ensure the bestowal and
reception of grace; and that even the young may so harden
their hearts in the midst of religious privileges as to prove
that they have no part nor lot in this matter.   A parent's
grace cannot save the children, who must seek and obtain
the grace of God for themselves.

The worship which during David's reign was celebrated
in the sanctuary on Zion was a truer figure of our New
Testament worship than either the worship in the Tabernacle in the wilderness, or that in Solomon's gorgeous
temple on Moriah; because the Ark of the Covenant, while

lodged on Mount Zion, was not hedged about with those fences which guarded it so strictly at all other periods of its history. On Zion there were no outer and inner courts shutting out the worshippers. There was no space there for such a system of prohibitions. One would even gather that David, who was not of the chosen tribe of Levi, had immediate access to the Ark itself. He apparently had access to the Holy of Holies, which at other periods was forbidden to all except the high priest; and, if so, may not other devout worshippers also have had the same liberty of approach to the mercy-seat? In using David's psalms as the Church's standard of devotion, the child of God has no sense of being excluded from the Divine presence, but feels, on the contrary, that he is free to " draw near with a true heart."

No doubt sacrifices, which at that time were offered in the high place in Gibeon, and not in Zion, are mentioned in David's psalms; but usually such references indicate rather their insufficiency, or, indeed, their absence. In the 50th Psalm, which is by Asaph, David's chief musician, Jehovah is represented as saying, " I will take no bullock out of thy house, nor he-goats out of thy folds. Offer unto God thanksgiving." In the 51st Psalm David declares that " the sacrifices of God are a broken spirit : a broken and a contrite heart, O God, Thou wilt not despise. Thou delightest not in burnt-offerings "; and he closes this wonderful psalm by intimating that a time was approaching when God would be " pleased with the sacrifices of righteousness, with burnt-offering and whole burnt-offering," when they should " offer bullocks upon his altar." This was to take place after the walls of Jerusalem, in which such wide breaches had been made by the warrior-king, were rebuilt, which was done by Solomon (1 Kings xi. 27).

In connection with the worship conducted upon Mount Zion, it should also be noticed that Obed-edom and his sons, who were foreigners, ministered before the Ark, thus anticipating the time when the Gentile races should be brought into the Church, and should share the privileges of the covenant people.

It is noteworthy that it was from this hill that PRAISE FIRST ASCENDED TO THE MOST HIGH IN THE PUBLIC SERVICES OF THE SANCTUARY. The worship of the patriarchs had no praise associated with it ; nor had the worship instituted by Moses. So far as regards praise, whether vocal or instrumental, it was silent. The worshippers took no audible part in the service, which was conducted by the priests ; and the priests presented no offering of praise, for the blowing of the two silver trumpets in connection with the solemn feasts and new moons (Num. x. 10) cannot be called praise. These seem to have served the purpose of our church-bells announcing the celebration of Divine worship. But when David was raised up to reorganize the ritual of worship, he at once introduced the element of praise. Public praise was first presented to God on Mount Zion ; and it is noteworthy that it was inaugurated when the sanctuary had its abode in a house, indicating that praise is a natural and suitable adjunct of worship in the family. David was wonderfully fitted by his natural gifts for doing this service to the Church of God, of which he was such a distinguished member. Before his day there were a few sacred songs composed by godly persons endowed with poetical and musical tastes, such as Miriam and Moses, Hannah and Deborah ; but these are quite exceptional, and they do not seem to have been ever used in the regular worship of the sanctuary. But with David's advent there was a loud outburst of song ; and the manner in which he summons all nations of the earth to unite in praising Jehovah, shows that he knew that he was appointed to introduce into Divine worship a new element which was to form one of its constituent parts among all races of mankind, to the end of time. The praise that now "waited for God in Zion" in the sweet psalms of Israel's national singer, seems rapidly to have become celebrated among all the surrounding nations, for we find the Jews lamenting in their exile in Babylon that they that carried them into captivity "required of them mirth, saying, Sing us one of the songs of Zion"; to which they made the touching reply, "How shall we sing the Lord's song in a foreign land?"

The gift of music and song, which characterised David in such a pre-eminent degree, is found reappearing after many generations in the Virgin Mary; and is it not probable that the Son inherited this taste through his mother from this royal ancestor? It is told in the Gospel narrative that, on the black night of our Lord's betrayal, "after they had sung an hymn" they went out from the upper room to the Mount of Olives. While the Lord Jesus lived in the spirit and practice of prayer, He seems never to have engaged in this exercise along with his disciples, though He sometimes prayed in their presence. But if He never joined with them in prayer, on this evening it is stated that He united with them in singing those holy hymns of his royal progenitor which were always sung at the Paschal season. Is it not natural, then, to suppose that on this occasion He Himself led their praises, as He presided at their meal?

Is it too daring a suggestion that He who is represented in one of David's psalms as exclaiming, after his death and resurrection, "My praise shall be of Thee in the great congregation," may sometimes lead the praises of the vast congregation of his redeemed ones in glory, presenting to God in their name their united offering of praise? By Him, therefore, let us, as the joyful children of Zion, "offer the sacrifice of praise to God continually," that is, the fruit of our lips, giving thanks to his name.

We should also observe that it was on Mount Zion, in

those psalms that were first composed and first sung there, that RELIGION BECAME AN INTENSELY PERSONAL THING. On Mount Zion religion assumed the marked aspect of a matter between God and the individual soul. The Commandments proclaimed on Mount Sinai were indeed addressed to the individual, as is indicated by the use of the personal pronoun, "Thou"; but it was on Mount Zion that the individual first distinctly responded to these personal appeals. It is now that we encounter constantly the pronouns, "*I*," "*Mine*," "*Me*," "*Thou*," "*Thine*," "*Thee*"— those emphatic words which Luther called the "hands and feet" of the psalms. It is by the use of these pronouns that the worshipper comes to God, appropriates God, and possesses God, and all the blessings which God bestows.

David is the inspired teacher who gave this personal character to religion and worship. In the patriarchal and Mosaic dispensations the family, social, and national aspects of religion are given prominence to; but no one can use the Psalms of David without feeling that if religion is to be real it must be *personal*, and that this sense of a personal dealing between the soul and God must be present in public worship as well as in private devotion. For while many of these spiritual outbreathings take the form of secret communion of the soul with its God, a personal approach to God, and an individual wrestling with sin and all the powers of darkness, they were composed to be sung in public by the worshippers assembled on Mount Zion. If we are to derive benefit from our religious services, there must be in our use of them this blending of the personal with the public devotional exercises. Yet, from the sanctuary we must learn to carry these holy songs into retirement and solitude, and to pour out our hearts in secret, in these deep experimental utterances, into the ear of our Father who is in secret.

Mount Zion was also THE SITE OF THE THRONE OF

ISRAEL'S MONARCH. A divinely anointed king wielded his sceptre here, as Jehovah said, "Yet have I set my king upon my holy hill of Zion"; and here he exercised that administration which was typical of the kingly office of the Messiah, of whom it was predicted that He should "reign over the house of Jacob for ever," and that "of his kingdom there should be no end." Mount Zion, therefore, bears emphatic witness to Christ's crown, that truth regarding which "He witnessed a good confession before Pontius Pilate." On the Roman ruler's putting to Him the question, "Art Thou a King, then?" He replied, "Thou sayest that I am a King: for this end was I born, and for this cause came I into the world, that I should bear witness unto the truth."

The true Christian must, in his private life, acknowledge Christ as his Supreme Lord and Master, rendering to Him all loyal obedience in thought, speech, and conduct. But the fact that those who typified the Messiah in his kingly office were crowned on Mount Zion, and exercised supreme govrenment over the chosen people (who represented the Church of God in these early ages) from that hill, teaches us that CHRIST IS THE SOLE KING AND HEAD OF HIS CHURCH. The Church in all its branches is bound to render fealty to Him, and to see that she does not allow his royal sceptre to be wrested from Him by any human ruler, whether ecclesiastical or secular. His servants are still commissioned to uphold in the world the apostolic testimony that "*there is another King, one Jesus*," and that all authority and power are subject to Him. They must still bear upon their outspread banner the old legend, "*For Christ's Crown*," and render Him homage at once as King of saints and King of kings.

The present protection and final exaltation of his people, when they "shall sit with Him on his throne," and the ultimate subjugation of all his and their enemies, are secured by the royal prerogative of our Divine King; and though the world does not yet acknowledge his sovereignty—

> The crowning day is coming
> By-and-by.

As we descend the slopes of Zion, let me ask, Have you captured the strongholds of sin in your own heart and life? Are you doing what is in your power to promote the fear and worship of God in the family of which you may be a member?

Do you know what personal religion is? Do you find that the Psalms with their personal pronouns express your feelings? A Scotch judge, in giving before a learned society a sketch of the life of one of its younger members, in noticing that he had expressed himself as very fond of the Psalms, added that he always observed that a religious character based on the Psalms was a genuine one.

Do you practically acknowledge Jesus as Lord and King in your heart and conduct?

XIV

𝕸𝖔𝖚𝖓𝖙 𝕺𝖑𝖎𝖛𝖊𝖙

The Mount of
Tears and Partings.

2 SAMUEL xv. 30.

O LIVET is the well-known hill lying east of Jerusalem, from which it is separated by the valley of Jehosha-phat, through which flows the stream of Kedron. It overtops Mount Moriah, on which stood the temple, and which is directly opposite it, by some 300 feet. From early times it was celebrated for the number and luxuriance of its olive trees, from which it derived its name ; and in the days of Nehemiah it was also clothed with palms, pines, and other trees, while myrtles grew in the valley beneath it, as mentioned by Zechariah, and fig trees embowered the villages of Bethphage and Bethany just over its crest. It has three distinct summits, the northern of which was in later times named Scopus. The central, which is the high-est, is called the Mount of Ascension, on which was erected the Church of the Ascension, in memory of our Lord's departure. The southern summit bears the name of the Hill of Offence. Confining our present review to the scenes which are recorded in the Old Testament Scriptures, let us enquire what important religious lessons are taught us by these.

The first scene depicted upon this mountain is when King David fled from his capital on the outbreak of the rebellion headed by his son Absalom. We are told that, having crossed the brook Kedron, "he went up by the ascent of Olivet, and wept as he went up, and had his head covered, and he went barefoot ; and all the people that was with him covered every man his head, and they went up, weeping as they went up." From the principal scenes on Olivet being associated with partings and with tears, the hill might be named the Mount of Partings.

The first incident in David's flight over this hill exhibits THE STEDFASTNESS OF TRUE LOYALTY AND AFFECTION as worthy of the highest praise (2 Sam. xv. 18–22). King David, like "great David's greater Son," had a wonderful power of attracting the loyal love of his followers. How staunch and true to him were these 600 foreigners from Gath, who, under their captain, Ittai the Gittite, formed the trusty bodyguard of the monarch, who in his early days of exile had sojourned within their territory. With characteristic unselfish regard for their interests, the king urged them to return to Jerusalem, because they were strangers and exiles. Their reply is worthy of being enshrined along with that of Ruth to Naomi, " Ittai answered the king, As the Lord liveth, and as my lord the king liveth, surely in what place my lord the king shall be, whether in death or life, even there also will thy servant be." It recalls the testimony borne by David's great Descendant to his followers, the tried and true, when, on the night when He crossed the same stream for the last time, He said to them, " Ye are they which have continued with Me in my temptations " ; while close to this very spot He evinced a similar disinterested love, when He said to the armed men who surrounded Him, " If ye seek Me, let these go their way."

But while the Mount of Olivet witnesses to the noble fidelity of true hearts, it also bears as emphatic witness to THE FEARFUL TREACHERY OF WHICH HUMAN NATURE IS CAPABLE.

Ahithophel and Judas are the world's two arch-traitors. Strange to tell, they both appear on the tragic page of history on this same hill. For it was as David was ascending its slopes that one brought him the disquieting news,

"Ahithophel is among the conspirators"; and the piety of the monarch is beautifully exhibited when, before he took measures to counteract the base treachery of his most trusted counsellor, he ejaculated the petition, "O Lord, I pray Thee, turn the counsel of Ahithophel into foolishness."

It was near the very spot where the Levites under Zadok set down the Ark of the Covenant on the ground, beside the Kedron, until the people who wept with a loud voice had passed over, that a thousand years later, Judas came up to Jesus, saying, "Hail, Master!" and kissed Him; for this was the signal which he had given to his fellow-conspirators, when he said, "Whomsoever I shall kiss, that same is He; hold Him fast!" History contains no blacker record of treachery than that of these two men, of whom the earlier was a prototype of the later—so that the words spoken regarding him by his innocent victim were afterwards appropriated to the Victim of Gethsemane: "We took sweet counsel together; we walked to the House of God in company. Yea, mine own familiar friend in whom I trusted, which did eat of my bread, hath lifted up his heel against Me." As we listen to our Lord, "troubled in spirit," saying to the Twelve, "Verily, I say unto you that one of you shall betray Me," does it not well become us, with searching of heart, to reply, "Lord, is it I?"

Hardly had David passed the top of Olivet, when a second instance of black treachery presented itself to him, in the arrival of Ziba with two asses bearing two hundred loaves of bread, a hundred bunches of rasins, a hundred of summer fruits, and a skin of wine, for the use of those who might become faint in the wilderness, while he accused his crippled master, Mephibosheth, the son of Jonathan, to whom David had shown such kindness, of aiming at the throne. Whether Ziba acted the part of a foul traducer of his master, or whether the latter acted the part of a base traitor to the king, who in his generosity had assigned him a constant place at his own table, is not clear.   David himself, by his decision that Mephibosheth and Ziba should share the estates that had belonged to Saul, avoided the painful investigation which would have been necessary to arrive at the truth.   This indicates that cases do occur in which prudence counsels a settlement which may leave a question of innocence or guilt in a state of dubiety, and the aggrieved party must await his vindication in providence, or at the Great Tribunal.

Such exhibitions of treachery, following immediately on the monstrous and unnatural conduct of Absalom towards his loving and too-indulgent father, amply prove the truth of the Divine verdict that the human heart is "deceitful above all things and desperately wicked."

The grief of the fugitive monarch, and his tears which fell so profusely on the rocky road over Olivet, were caused not only by the painful circumstances of his flight, but by the prospect of being separated from the Ark of God.   For he had bidden Zadok and the Levites carry back the symbol of Jehovah's gracious presence to Jerusalem, saying, "If I shall find favour in the eyes of the Lord, He will bring me again, and show me both it and his habitation.   But if He say thus, I have no delight in thee; behold, here am I, let Him do to me as seemeth good unto Him!"   In the whole range of literature there are few passages more touching than David's utterances of his LONGING FOR THE PRIVILEGE OF AGAIN JOINING GOD'S PEOPLE IN PUBLIC WORSHIP.

> My soul is pourèd out in me
>   When this I think upon,
> Because that with the multitude
>   I heretofore had gone.
>
> With them into God's house I went
>   With voice of joy and praise,
> Yea, with the multitude that kept
>   The solemn, holy days.

Oh, why art thou cast down, my soul?
　Why in me so dismay'd?
Trust God, for I shall praise Him yet,
　His countenance is mine aid.—*Psa. xlii. 4, 5.*

But though now debarred from the public ordinances of grace, he did not on this account cease to engage in such exercises of worship as were still open to him, for it is recorded that "when David was come to the top of the mount, he worshipped God." Are we careful to follow his example in this? And when we are providentially prevented from going to the House of God, do we cherish the worshipper's spirit, and ENGAGE IN PRIVATE EXERCISES OF DEVOTION? Do we worship God on our journeys, even on the wayside, as David did? In the absence of visible and assuring tokens of Jehovah's presence, he still sought his face. Let us also, in default of the faith of assurance, see that we exercise the faith of adherence.

Passing from the reign of David to that of his son, we learn that on this hill of Olivet Solomon built shrines " for Chemosh, the abomination of Moab, and for Molech, the abomination of the children of Ammon," and for the idols of other nations with whom he had contracted matrimonial alliances (1 Kings xi. 7). Alas, that this hill should have borne witness to the cooling of the first devotion and love of him who in his youth made such a noble request that the Lord would give him "an understanding heart, that he might discern between good and bad"—the hill itself now receiving the name of the Mount of Corruption! We are reminded that THE SIN OF BACKSLIDING besets even those who from their youth have been ardent in the Lord's service; and that worldly prosperity, and entangling connections and friendships, not formed in the fear of God, tend seriously to lower piety, and to corrupt the whole-heartedness of our religion.

The fact that these idolatrous high-places remained till they were destroyed by the reforming zeal of the good King

Josiah, 350 years later, reminds us that "the evil that men do lives after them," and that it is hard to compute what far-reaching influences our evil doings may exert upon others, even upon future generations. How sad if our Olivets of beauty, and of tender associations, should be changed by our faults into Mounts of Corruption and Hills of Offence!

The next scene upon Olivet in sacred story is when the prophet Ezekiel, carried in vision by the Spirit of the Lord from Babylon to Jerusalem, saw the Shechinah-glory which he had watched leaving its abode over the Cherubim, and its temporary station on the threshold of the Temple, standing on the Mount of Olives preparatory to its final quitting of the Holy City. By withdrawing the symbol of his Presence from his Temple and his people, the Lord taught his Church that HE WILL NOT CONTINUE TO DWELL WITH THOSE WHO FORSAKE HIS LAWS. The Psalmist had enquired, "Lord, who shall abide in thy tabernacle? Who shall dwell in thy holy hill?" And the response, given alike by the Lord and by his own conscience, was, "He that hath clean hands and a pure heart." If his professing people become unrighteous, and impure in character, and false and formal in their religion, God will forsake them. No Church can afford to rest in an honoured history and sacred traditions; nor is any individual safe in trusting to his past experience and reputation.

The wise man had "seen the wicked buried who had come and gone from the place of the holy, and they were forgotten in the city where they had so done." Oblivion swallowed up these worshippers and their vain religious performances, and their place and means of grace were left to those who would make a better use of them. The Lord said to Ezekiel concerning such persons, " They come unto thee as the people cometh, and they sit before thee as my people, and they hear thy words, but they will not do them; for with their mouth they show much love, but their heart goeth after their covetousness. And, lo, thou art unto them as a very lovely song, of one that hath a pleasant voice, and can play well on an instrument; for they hear thy words, but they do them not." The Lord will still withdraw his presence from all who frequent the sanctuary attracted only by the eloquence or argumentative skill of the preacher, the beauty of the music, or the decorum of the services, or who use religious worship as a spiritual narcotic to lull the conscience into a fatal slumber, instead of coming to church to seek God's presence, and to hear his message with the purpose of carrying it out in practice.

Olivet reminds us that He dealt thus with the Jews, and we may be assured that He will not act otherwise towards professing Christians. Their holy House shall be left desolate unto all such—either a heap of ruins, or an empty shell from which the glory has departed.

Another impressive and instructive scene took place on this mount when the Jews, who had returned from their long captivity in Babylon to the land of their fathers, went out to Olivet, and fetched olive branches, and pine branches, and myrtle branches, and palm branches, and branches of thick trees to make booths, that they might keep the Feast of Tabernacles as it was written (Neh. viii. 13–15). We are taught here THE IMPORTANCE OF KEEPING OUR HOLY FEAST according to its institution. It was a stirring scene that day on Olivet when the people made preparations to keep this feast; but if their hands were busy and their bodies fatigued, their hearts were happy. The sorrow that had clouded them when they heard the law read by the Levites, and learned how remiss they had been in conforming to its injunctions, was now dispelled. "Hold your peace!" the Levites had cried to the weeping crowds; "neither be ye sorry, for the joy of the Lord is your strength." When they had made ready their feast, and sent "portions to those for whom nothing was prepared," and had taken up their temporary abode in the booths woven from the trees of Olivet, remembering that their true and settled home was not on earth, but in heaven, then, we are told, " there was very great gladness." In like manner, the due observance of our great New Testament Feast is obligatory upon all. Its neglect is sinful, and we must keep it, remembering that we are pilgrims and strangers on earth, and seek for a short season to disengage ourselves from the cares and anxieties, the secular pursuits and pleasures of life ; and so we, too, shall be glad as we think upon our eternal home above.

The last reference to Olivet in the Old Testament (and the scope of this volume precludes us from extending our view to the New Testament incidents connected with it), tells us that the Lord will return again to the world and to his waiting people—to the world in judgment, to his people in abounding mercy. The prophet Zechariah writes (chap. xiv. 4), " Behold the day of the Lord cometh, . . . and his feet shall stand in that day upon the Mount of Olives, which is before Jerusalem on the east." This prediction directly refers to our Lord's Second Advent.

The Lord Jesus selected this hill as the spot from which He would ascend to his Father in heaven. It was endeared to Him by many associations. He had thrice wet its soil with his tears. At Bethany, on its eastern side, He wept, as in company with Mary and Martha He slowly approached the tomb of their brother Lazarus. He wept in sympathy with the weeping sisters, and under his own sense of the insatiable cruelty of the grave in snatching away a loved friend, even though He was about to recall him from that mysterious bourne from which no traveller returns, but of whose remorseless gates He holds the keys. As David crossing Olivet wept when he left his home and its sanctuary, hardly daring to hope that he should return again, so the Son of David wept bitter tears as from the ridge of the same hill He gazed with the affection of a patriot, the deep concern of a prophet, and his own unfathomable Divine pity, upon the capital of his country, the city of his nation's solemnities, and the scene of his own fast-approaching sufferings and death.   And we are also told (Heb. v. 7) that in the garden at the foot of this mount "He offered up prayers and supplications with strong crying and tears unto Him that was able to save Him from death."

We do not wonder that Jesus chose this hill as the spot where He should take farewell of earth, and carry away from it his last view of the land He loved so well; and is it not as true to his human nature, that when He returns to our earth He should arrive upon this same hill?   "Ye men of Galilee," said the two angels in white apparel to the awe-struck disciples, as a cloud received their loved Master from their sight, "why stand ye gazing up into heaven?   This same Jesus which is taken up from you into heaven, shall so come as ye have seen Him go into heaven" (Acts i. 9–12).

> Lo, He comes with clouds descending,
>   Once for favoured sinners slain ;
> Thousand thousand saints attending,
>   Swell the triumph of his train.

Olivet bids all Christians to remember that THEIR LORD IS COMING AGAIN.   His Church has often mistaken the time, and perhaps, in some respects, the character of his return and of his kingdom, but there is nothing more sure than that Christ will return, and return to reign.   We are not to keep our eyes downcast in sorrow on the earth ; nor are we to stand gazing up and scanning the heavens with too curious enquiry and calculation, but we are to return to our worship and our work, assured that our Lord will come again.   And since we know neither the day nor the hour of his Coming, it behoves us to be as men waiting for the return of their Lord, with our loins girt and our lamps

burning, not knowing whether He will come in the evening,
or at midnight, or at the cock-crowing, or in the morning.

Our heart shall then rejoice, for we shall see Him again,
and our joy no man shall take from us. And when He
returns for the eternal redemption of his people, when
his feet stand once more upon the Mount of Olives, surely
his Church gathered together from the four winds and from
one end of heaven to the other, will welcome Him with a
loud acclaim, like that which the multitude going before
and following Him with their palm-branches raised, as He
descended the slope of Olivet long ago : " Hosanna to the
Son of David ! Blessed is He that cometh in the name of
the Lord : Hosanna in the highest ! "

As we leave the Mount of Olives, with all its mingled
memories, let me ask you,

Do you value and wait on the public ordinances of
worship ?   Do you mourn under the privation of these
when, in Providence, you are shut out from them ? and do
you wait upon God in such ways as are still open to you ?

Are you convinced of the awful wickedness of your heart,
and of its native treachery, even towards your Saviour ?

Are you cleaving to the Lord, like David, or backsliding,
like Solomon ?

Do you bear in mind that the Lord will withdraw his
presence from all who render Him a worship that is in-
sincere ?

Are you waiting for the Second Coming of the Lord
Jesus, assured that He will return in his glory, and all his
holy angels with Him, " to be glorified in his saints, and to
be admired in all them that believe " ?